Secrets to

Barrel Racing

Success

Disclaimer

Dedication

To the horses who have gone through life misunderstood;

To the reader; a student of life, of horses, of horsemanship, and of barrel racing. May curiosity and confidence lead you to become all you were truly destined for.

Acknowledgments

To my mom, Janet:

Thank you for introducing me to horses and for providing a childhood miles removed from asphalt streets.

To my husband, Craig:

You have shown me what unconditional love really is. Thank you for your unwavering support and encouragement.

To my teachers:

While horses have been my greatest teachers, I am forever grateful to Jodi Greenley Lundberg, Holly Marsh, Lynn Kohr and Kim Kizzier for so kindly sharing their wisdom.

To my equine soul mate, Pistol:

Although he cannot read (yet), I must acknowledge my four-legged friend for his patience, honesty, try and forgiving nature. The partnership we share is an ongoing blessing. Pistol continues to show me that when I put the relationship first, anything is STILL possible.

In remembrance of my childhood mare, Gypsy:

Who taught me to NEVER GIVE UP.

Table of Contents

Throughout this book, I have used the pronouns "he" and "him" to refer to the singular barrel horse. In addition, I have assigned the pronouns "she" and "her" to the rider. I acknowledge, however, that barrel horses and barrel racers can be of either gender.

“ *If you keep on doing what you've always done, you'll keep on getting what you've always got.* **”**

– W. L. Bateman

Introduction

My Journey

Over 20 years ago, a harvested wheat field next to my rural North Dakota home seemed to be the perfect practice pen. I could be seen running my little mare around three plastic barrels in the stubble – over and over and over. Each run was not quite adequate in my mind. I would keep running again and again until I felt our trip around the pattern was perfect (which was rare). Little did I know the physical and mental wear and tear I was causing my mare. Little did I know we were solidifying bad habits and creating

blocks to success that would take years to realize and undo. Little did I know that we would never achieve success running barrels as long as I was so ignorant. What I was doing wasn't working, but I kept doing it anyway. In fact what I was doing was further distancing my mare and I from what I wanted so badly.

I kicked, I jerked, I spanked, I screamed, I cried (a lot), I even cussed! I experienced frustration of epic proportions, it seemed never-ending. We fought our way through the fog for many years together. Running her through the pattern over and over was just one of many mistakes I made. We'd make improvements only to put it to the test, and fail. And fail again. It was hard, it was exhausting, it was embarrassing, and it made me want to give up.

But I didn't.

I was not raised in a rodeo family, but caught the "horse bug" from my mother who had a horse growing up. I remember her saying "put your weight in your feet," and away I'd go. I clearly could have used more instruction than that. In the 1980's, in the heart of farm country, and on a shoe string budget, it was hard to come by. When I look back now, I see that my little green broke mare didn't come to me properly prepared to be a young girl's barrel horse, and although I'd been riding my pony since age four, I wasn't prepared to be a young barrel racer.

I can't look back with complete regret because there were valuable lessons I gained from my early experiences with horses; however, many of those experiences proved to be sidetracks on my road to barrel racing success. Subconscious fears were instilled within me that affected the way I rode and the way I thought. Deep down, I doubted myself and my abilities with horses. One layer at a time I have been gradually removing these blocks and clearing the path to the success I have wanted for so long.

Photo © Kandi Schuman Photography

I now reflect back with gratitude for that firecracker of a mare. She left me with a toolbox full of problem solving techniques that I continue to utilize today. Growing up so far removed from an equestrian lifestyle has actually created a deep appreciation for my current reality. I am now thankful for my humble beginnings, which required me to learn out of necessity to start colts before I could be serious about barrel racing. On the edges of the clouds that darkened my early experiences was a beautiful, shimmering gold lining – lessons and gifts that have impacted me in a positive way, to a much greater extent than I have allowed those negative experiences hold me back.

66 *When you know better you do better.* 99

– Maya Angelou

As the years went on, horses came and went. I spent time studying, collecting information, researching, applying, testing, and experimenting through trial and error. If the frustration I felt as a child was acute, it could be said that I spent many more years in a state of chronic frustration. Just as I started to think I had something figured out, or had possibly found the one "missing piece" to my barrel racing puzzle, I would realize that there were still many pieces nowhere to be found. The search continued.

BARREL RACING SUCCESS

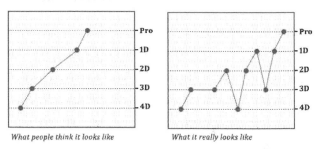

What people think it looks like   *What it really looks like*

Upon receiving some bit of advice, instruction or information, I would often find myself even more confused. Was I really that dense? Or was it possible that the information could be presented in a way that was more easily understood and applied? When I finally figured out what the individual was trying to get across, I'd think to myself, "Why didn't they just *say that*!?" At other times, I would wonder, "*Why* would they leave that out!?" when considering some crucial bit of information, necessary for the success of a certain maneuver or technique. The gaps were significant – no wonder I had been struggling for so long.

There were a few years in which I put barrel racing on the back burner to focus on training for and competing in reining events, on horses that (I realize now) didn't even have an aptitude for the discipline. Because my options were limited, I found myself taking on numerous troubled horses. Rather than question my judgment, I have recognized that what I gained from those experiences has played, and continues to play, a huge part in my success as a barrel racer.

Even though I now choose to embrace my past experiences with gratitude, it's not a route I can recommend. When I look back on the early years, it seems so obvious that I was sabotaging my own success. It is my assumption, or at least my hope, that most barrel racers have not and will not experience the degree of frustration that I did. There is much more information available today than there was twenty years ago. The gaps in the puzzle do not have to be so great; the clouds do not have to be so dark.

More often than not, however, we go forward in life with a puzzle full of holes without even knowing it, which would be much like running the barrel pattern, kicking and whipping to beat the band, not realizing we are holding back on the reins. I laugh when I visualize that picture – imagine your barrel buddy screaming from the fence *"Let GO of the REINS!"*

The reality is that on some level we all do this, we all have weak areas in our horsemanship, or within ourselves, that hold us back. The reality also, is that our horses don't think it's funny. Fortunately, they are tolerant and forgiving animals. Fortunately, if we look hard enough, and in the right places, we can find what is needed to strengthen those weak areas.

❝ *No matter what happens, no matter how far you seem to be away from where you want to be, never stop believing that you will somehow make it. Have an unrelenting belief that things will work out, that the long road has purpose, that the things that you desire may not happen today, but they will happen. Continue to persist and persevere.* ❞

— Brad Gast

My Desire

Today's world operates at a whirlwind pace. I realize your "barrel racer hat" is likely to be one of many you wear. With respect to your multiple life responsibilities, I want to give you the best results for your time and monetary commitment. Quite simply, I have cut out the fluff. Did you know that most book contracts state a certain number of words that the author must agree to? I am happy to report, that is not the case here. I have only filled this book with quality, easy to understand, but hard to find information necessary not just to train and maintain a barrel horse, but intended to help you achieve *real results*. Over the years I have gained insights from a wide variety of teachers and experiences. These unique and valuable insights – only those that have *made a real positive difference* – have made it onto the following pages.

Secrets to Barrel Racing Success is different than any other resource available to barrel racers. As you read, you will be challenged to develop new awareness and ways of thinking. My wish is to help lift your dark clouds and give you some clues to find missing pieces in your own puzzle. I want to provide light on your individual path to barrel racing success and invite you to release your grip on the reins. When you equip yourself with knowledge and develop more clarity and confidence, you will receive a new kind of enjoyment from barrel racing, an enjoyment you quite possibly haven't experienced up to this point.

It is my sincere intention to help horses and barrel racers, not just avoid unnecessary suffering, stress and frustration (which might only leave you coasting in neutral), but actually realize the presence of blocks that are standing in the way of success and dissolve them, opening up new pathways to WINNING in the process. I realize now when I look back at my life that all the experiences through which I developed and then dissolved *my own* blocks and opened up a path to the success I always wanted, was for a purpose. This is it.

Secrets to Barrel Racing Success is the result of my personal journey so far.

Thank you for taking the ride with me,

Heather Smith

❝ *Even if you're on the right track, you'll get run over if you just sit there.* **❞**

— Will Rogers

How to Benefit

As we begin, I would like to describe some qualities of the readers I envision *Secrets to Barrel Racing Success* being of the most value to, and what can be done to gain the maximum benefit from the information on the following pages.

It seems like some of us "horse folk" have a tendency to get stuck in our ways and repeat the same old methods and techniques, even if there are new ones that work much better and are readily available for us. The western world is one that values tradition, but being a successful barrel racer means knowing when to release the attachments to traditions that aren't in our best interest. Being successful means opening one's mind to new ways of doing and perceiving things and recognizing what techniques and ideas actually hinder progress more than they help. Some of the basic principles of horsemanship are timeless, but at the same time,

many methods that were acceptable and achieved results ten years ago are outdated today. Those who are committed to being the best are open to change. They are willing to consider and implement new methods of training and horse care that are the most effective and beneficial.

Many barrel racers today still live by the code of the west. Not discouraged by hard work, we stand for principles such as honesty, integrity and courage. The physical labor and expenses involved in caring for, traveling with and competing on 1,200 lb. animals is not something most people are willing or able to take on. Generally it can be said that we are action takers. We take actions and make sacrifices every day to make horses and barrel racing part of our lives.

As competitors we possess an inner drive to excel, to continuously better ourselves and our horses. Chances are you are unwilling to settle for mediocrity. Not believing in doing anything half heartedly, you give your best effort to whatever you set out to do. The fact that this book made it into your hands suggests that you are interested in continuous learning and self-development.

There is a fearlessness and freedom that barrel racers share. Why hold back when you could be blasting down the alley? You set your standards high and rather than hoping and wishing and making excuses, you develop an action plan to achieve your desires and go for it. These are all great qualities and characteristics, but even more important than action, is *implementation*.

> 66 *Knowing is not enough; we must apply. Willing is not enough; we must do.* 99
>
> — Johann Wolfgang von Goethe

As barrel racers, we understand there is no achievement without forward movement. But forward movement alone is not enough, it must be *quality* forward movement. It's not so much *knowledge*, but *what we do* with our knowledge, that determines our success.

We all have a similar basic goal – to WIN. The paths we each take to get there will vary. Your education, as it applies to barrel racing, can and will come from many different sources. If I had one suggestion to help receive the most benefit from this book, it would be to carefully consider the contents, and think of it as part of a solid, but integrative foundation.

A second book in the BarrelRacingTips.com series, featuring barrel racing exercises, is likely to play an important role in your journey as well. If winning is our destination, and exercises part of the journey, then *Secrets to Barrel Racing Success* is a prerequisite to everything else, yet far beyond the basics. This book delivers the message that the *way* in which we *implement* exercises (or any other part of our program) is *far more critical* to our success than *action alone*. The content in the pages that follow provide a solid foundation not only to fall back on, but from which to base the development of your horse *and* yourself.   It's not the foundation you may be thinking of though, it's deeper than that. As you'll soon find out, this book truly contains the little known *Secrets to Barrel Racing Success*.

Only when you stop going through the motions and start understanding how a solid foundation can set you up to succeed, whether you're sacrificing the relationship with your horse, what it means to have true awareness and feel, the importance of proper timing and foot placement, rider positioning, quality of

Photo © www.CowboyImages.net

movement, responsiveness under all circumstances, horse health and well being, and your inner game, are you likely to truly benefit from this book, or any other resource.

By sinking into the contents of this book, you will set yourself up to receive much more as you go forward. For example, many of the exercises contained in the second volume of the BarrelRacingTips.com series are tried and true, having been used to develop winning barrel horses for years.   Some will seem unfamiliar and may even find you initially questioning how they would apply to barrel racing. What makes *Secrets to Barrel Racing Success* unique is the *way* in which I recommend you go about implementing exercises, which is through utilizing horsemanship methods that work *with* the horse's tendencies rather than against them.   Regardless of the discipline, when we learn ways of communicating that horses instinctively understand, the human *and* the horse win. Although we all have similar goals, the path we take and the *way* in which we travel *matters,* and directly affects the results we achieve.

Above and Beyond

We've determined that as competitors and as barrel racers, we have a desire for something greater. My challenge for you is to take your quest for excellence to a higher level. In the process you will be challenged to shift your thinking and perceptions, and maybe even throw out old ways of doing things, with the new found belief that "because it's always been done that way" is no longer good enough. I invite you to go forward *willing* to change, fail, experiment, question and especially, succeed.

Through this process a firm foundation of confidence will be created. Not a "know it all" confidence but a contentedness in qualities you currently possess as a barrel racer, a contentedness in your place on the journey and yet an open mind to the ever presenting opportunities to add to your knowledge and skills. Developing this foundation empowers you to sort out sometimes conflicting information, determine what truly resonates with you and make decisions you can stand firm in. You can go forward, not being easily swayed by outside influences, and can rest knowing that at every opportunity you did your very best to provide the highest level of care and education possible to your horses. Do your homework, and you can compete and look back with satisfaction rather than regret.

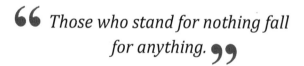 *Those who stand for nothing fall for anything.*

— Alex Hamilton

Barrel racing at a high level will always require hard work and a commitment to continuous self-development. There are likely to be bumps in the road, and the truth is, we may never have ALL the pieces to the puzzle. There will always be room for improvement and gaps in our horsemanship can exist no matter how much we have already achieved. The paths of development we follow are often spiral in nature. This book, if read again in five years, may have a totally new meaning for you. As you study and gain experiences in certain areas, you are likely to return to those same areas again down the road, taking your learning and growth to a deeper level.

It's my suggestion that you integrate at least five things from this book before moving on to the next one. This is a good policy to have for every piece of educational material you dive into. Although I hope you'll take away many more than five concepts, make a promise to yourself to choose at least five key points to integrate, remembering that we often resist what we need most. As a result, rather than just reading about barrel racing success, you may soon find yourself experiencing it.

As you go forward, may your unwavering commitment to self-development help smooth out your personal road to barrel racing success and provide much satisfaction and enjoyment as you're traveling.

Intellectuals solve problems; geniuses prevent them.

— Albert Einstein

Create a Solid Foundation

The House You Build

Not every barrel racer has "horse trainer" on their resume; however, as riders, we are also trainers. Every interaction we have with a horse is shaping them for the better or for the worse. This is both a responsibility to be aware of and an opportunity to take advantage of.

The importance of a solid foundation in our horse's training is often emphasized. In recent years, effective training techniques have become more readily available to the masses. Combine that with specialized barrel horse breeding programs and it's safe to say that the competition is tougher than it's ever been. A serious barrel racer can't afford to be at a disadvantage; yet it is a common occurrence to witness examples of an educational foundation missing in young and old horses alike.

In this section I'd like to get clear on *why* a solid foundation is important. Throughout this book you'll have the opportunity to better understand what constitutes a truly solid foundation. Attempting to compete without an adequate educational foundation puts the "cart before the horse." You will be going nowhere fast, and we all know that is not the goal!

A common metaphor compares the solid foundation necessary in a young horse to that of a house. If there are holes or cracks in the foundational structure of a building, it will not hold up in the long run. Stuck with the time consuming and expensive chore of trying to repair the foundation, frustration grows as other parts of the house also become damaged due to the faulty base. Over time, instead of standing firm to the elements and wear, the foundation continually weakens, requiring additional repairs and damage to other parts of the home, possibly even causing it to eventually crumble to the ground.

No matter how excited you might be to move into a new house, you would agree that it would not be wise to authorize the builders to neglect processes that strengthen the home's foundation. If you choose to skip over important steps just to enjoy the finished product sooner, you're likely to be extremely disappointed when in no time you have to complete major repairs or maybe even rebuild completely. The same goes for starting a colt or ensuring an older horse has a proper education. Being thorough the first time is always a worthwhile investment. Building a strong foundation in a house *or* a horse can make all the difference when it comes to the success and longevity we (and the horse) enjoy as a result.

If a problem crops up on the barrel pattern, addressing the issue requires much less time and effort when there are solid basics to fall back on. With less correction required, your horse is also less likely to develop resentment toward the barrel pattern. Without a solid foundation, fixing a problem is not only difficult, it might even be impossible. In some cases a horse must be completely brought back to the basics to build the foundation up where it was lacking. This unfortunate situation is discouraging to any horse and rider.

Colt starting doesn't have to be "western."

When considering the speed and exhilaration of competition, it's understandable how it would be tempting to skip over certain steps in a hurry to achieve the end result. When we realize what we are up against without a solid foundation in place, and that going forward without it is likely to delay our success even further, we are empowered to make better choices.

Although this is a great metaphor, and although it's not always appropriate to assign human emotions to animals, I would like to compare the importance of instilling a proper educational foundation in our horses to that of doing the same for a child. After all, we are not dealing with inanimate structures, but intelligent, living, breathing, feeling (sometimes 1,200 lb.) animals.

The Future is In Our Hands

Humor me if you will and visualize a little boy in school, let's say first grade. His name is Billy and the teacher has asked the class to write a short sentence. Billy's mother has looked forward to the day when he graduates college and becomes a huge success. In fact, she's so anxious that she authorized him to skip kindergarten. Billy would love to write a sentence but without having first attended kindergarten, he doesn't even know the ABC's. Below I've mapped out three scenarios to show examples of what can happen when a child (or horse) does or does not have the all-important educational foundation in place.

Scenario #1

Billy's first grade teacher places high priority on the completion of assignments. Billy doesn't seem to focus on his work, so he is the recipient of a stern talking to. He feels guilty, but deep down, he is totally confused. Rather than be concerned with WHY Billy is struggling, the teacher's main focus continues to be that he completes the tasks he has been given.

As the years go by, Billy continues to struggle and teachers have classified him as "special needs" and classmates have even labeled him "stupid." The truth is, Billy is actually quite bright, willing and talented; however, the less others believe in him, the less he believes in himself. Billy is constantly discouraged by the difficulties he experiences that all link back to never having been properly taught the alphabet.

With nothing but negative experiences to associate with school, Billy loses interest and eventually drops out. Unable to get a job, Billy turns to stealing and drugs to make a living and to cope with his feelings of inadequacy. His mother's dreams for him are dashed. He travels down a very unfortunate road for someone who once had such a promising future.

Scenario #2

When Billy starts 6th grade, a sensitive, compassionate teacher takes special interest in understanding his shortcomings. It becomes obvious to her why he struggles with reading and comprehending when he doesn't even have a full understanding of spelling and writing. She spends extra time with Billy after school every day for the entire year. With each small success, his self-worth grows. He still experiences difficulties at times but the future is looking much brighter for young Billy. He eventually graduates high school, then college and enjoys a long, successful career.

Scenario #3

An understanding, intuitive teacher is present just as Billy starts first grade. She finds out that he was inappropriately authorized to skip kindergarten. Before going any further Billy is assigned a special tutor to catch him up on all the basics of the alphabet. In no time he is completing his assignments with flying colors. The students and teachers see him as the intelligent, talented student that he is. He goes through school always ranking at the top of his class and eventually completes medical school and spends his life performing critical surgeries on less-fortunate children.

As a small child, it was no fault of his own that Billy did not receive a proper educational foundation. At his age, it was up to the adults in his life to take responsibility to set him up to succeed. From the time he was born, Billy's mother had dreamed of him becoming a big success. Although she meant well, she didn't realize the effect that skipping kindergarten would have.

Regardless of whether you are playing the important role of teacher or have chosen a professional trainer to assist in educating your horse, remember that the rest of their lives will be shaped by whether they receive a proper educational foundation. In addition, each person who comes into contact with that horse as long as he lives will be affected as well, either positively or negatively.

The first 30 rides are a critical stage of development.

Now I realize that chances of your horse doing drugs or performing surgery is slim. All kidding aside, we can choose to be part of a problem or part of a solution. Why not give youngsters (horse or human) a chance to become positive, productive members of society and assist those older students who weren't as fortunate in their more formative years? Each of us holds the power in our hands to make the horse world a better place for future generations.

But what if you just want to WIN, like, aaahhhh...NOW!?

My message doesn't waver in this instance. Remember the disadvantages of skipping over important parts of the home building process? A proper educational foundation will set our horses up to win, in more ways than one. When our horses understand how to lightly yield to pressure, to stay respectfully between our reins and legs, to collect or lengthen their stride just by responding to our subtle body language, then learning to efficiently navigate the barrel pattern comes with ease.

A horse that wins consistently is a horse that *loves running barrels.* Develop a positive association with learning, with the barrels and with people in general by doing your very best to provide a thorough foundation before even considering taking a trip around the cloverleaf pattern. A lot of horses with potential never succeed in competition because they weren't started properly. Quite simply, the odds are more in your favor to develop a *winning* barrel horse, if you take the time it takes to build a strong foundation *first.*

When we truly understand horses, we are not so quick to judge and label a misbehaving one as an "idiot," or "naughty," or blame them for not performing on the barrel pattern correctly. Solving problems becomes much easier when we realize that issues are nearly always linked to something missing in the foundation. Look to yourself as a teacher and leader first. What is the *real underlying reason* the horse is responding in a way *we perceive* as undesirable? Where are there weak areas in the horse's educational foundation? How could you do a better job of improving those areas? What *letters of the alphabet* does this horse still need to learn before he can even consider *making a sentence?*

> **❝** *When a man points a finger at someone else, he should remember that four of his fingers are pointing at himself.* **❞**

– Louis Nizer

You might wonder just what constitutes a proper educational foundation for a barrel horse? I'll start by saying that a foundation is really more than education. Let's face it, much of what a child needs to learn to thrive in this world is not provided at school. As we develop our horses, we want to make sure we're also helping them develop a mental and emotional foundation that will serve them and make their life as a performance horse easier. A true horseman is mindful to develop all of these areas of the foundation at the same time.

From an educational stand point, we could generalize and say that we should expect the basics listed below from a horse after 60 days of quality foundational training. Of course this can vary depending on the individual horse.

1. Respectfully move forward to lead when asked by the handler on the ground
2. Be tied and stand quietly when tied

3. Pick up all four feet well enough to be trimmed without resistance
4. Willingly load and unload from a horse trailer
5. Laterally flex the neck and yield hindquarters on the ground
6. Vertical flexion and backing on the ground
7. Lunge in both directions with impulsion at all gaits with smooth transitions
8. Accept the saddle and bridle without avoidance
9. Stand quietly for mounting
10. Laterally flex the neck and yield hindquarters under saddle
11. Vertical flexion and backing under saddle
12. Carry rider in both directions at all gaits with fairly smooth transitions
13. A beginner understanding of yielding to leg pressure

After a basic foundation is established, further development builds on these basic understandings. Remember that the process doesn't look like the product. Had I known this when I was a kid, I would have realized that running my horse on the pattern over and over was not going to result in better performance. Put horsemanship before sportsmanship; the more advanced a horse's foundational training, the easier they will take to the barrel pattern. Generally, before starting specific training for barrel racing, we should expect the horse to:

1. Uphold the responsibility to maintain gait on a straight line or circle
2. Stop smoothly when the rider relaxes and sits deep in the saddle
3. Transition easily up and down between gaits in response to subtle body language
4. Uphold the responsibility to maintain direction on a straight line or circle
5. Remain focused and responsive to rider in differing environments and circumstances

6. Move rib cage laterally to leg pressure from a standstill and at the walk, trot and lope
7. Move shoulder laterally to leg pressure from a standstill and at the walk, trot and lope
8. Move hip laterally to leg pressure from a standstill and at the walk, trot and lope
9. Pick up the right or left lead on a straight line when cued by the rider
10. Be willing guided in circles of different size and speed
11. Laterally and vertically flex and yield the body parts (neck, shoulder, rib and hip) in various directions and at various gaits in isolation or combination
12. Travel in a collected manner and have a beginner ability to maintain self carriage
13. Maintain emotional control and mental focus when traveling at moderate speed

The chapter titled *Are You Ready?* at the end of this book includes a quiz that can give you some insight into how strong your foundation is, and determine whether you have the prerequisites in place that are necessary for success in the barrel racing arena. Providing the intricacies of developing a solid educational foundation in book form alone would be extremely difficult to say the least, and that is not the specific purpose of this book. Fortunately there are many excellent trainers and clinicians that offer resources (books, clinics, DVD's, etc.) for learning the how-to's involved in this process that will help you further your education in this area.

Whether you have children, horses or both, if you are human, you are likely to be familiar with the fact that we all make mistakes. Even though we may believe we are instilling solid foundations in our horses, that foundation could be full of holes and cracks that we are not even aware of. Mistakes, however, can be perceived as positive when we learn from them, apply the lessons and do better next time.

❝ You can never make the same mistake twice. The second time you make it, it's no longer a mistake. It's a choice. ❞

– Unknown

Because it's not uncommon to recognize examples of this lack of foundation, we might even get caught in a comparison game. It's important to keep in mind, that although we may have a more solid foundation than some or even most others, it's no excuse for not working to further develop our own. I haven't known anyone who achieved excellence in any area by measuring themselves against the lowest common denominator. As long as you have an open mind and are committed to self-development you will keep discovering ways in which you and your horse can grow and build an even more solid foundation.

Becoming a winning barrel racer is certainly a goal worth pursuing. We spend enormous amounts of time on preparation compared to the little time spent actually competing, which of course is the highlight. As you go forward, don't let the attraction to competition and winning convince you to rush though critical prerequisites. In your haste, you will actually be creating blocks and delays on your path to achieving your loftiest goals.

By instilling a solid foundation in a young horse or strengthening that of an older horse, you are sure to reap rewards – in the form of more wins *and* in a contribution to the greater good of horses and the barrel racing industry as a whole.

66 *Seek first to understand, then to be understood.* **99**

— Stephen Covey

Build a Relationship

Getting Over the Gap

Have you ever run a three legged race? If so, you know that it can be so difficult that many people find watching others even try hysterical!   Participating in such a race can go a little more smoothly when you are able to communicate with your partner and develop a race plan.   Even in that case you're still likely to experience difficulties – often times the members of a team get out of sync, resulting in one or both falling down.

Humor me for a moment, and imagine being paired up in a three (five) legged race with a deer.   You might think – *Ha, IMPOSSIBLE!* Of course, it's easy to make that judgment because most humans don't speak "deer."   If you did speak the same language, and could communicate in a way the deer would easily understand, it would open up an entire world of possibilities for gaining cooperation.

Now imagine saddling a deer. You can guess at what the result might look like, and it's not pretty. Of course, your intention would not be to harm the deer.   In the last few million years, however, he's developed instincts that make it difficult to convince him otherwise. A human asking for connection and cooperation from a deer, is very comparable to asking the same thing of a horse, whose brain operates in much the same way. Deer and horses, both prey animals operating on instincts, have one goal that rises above all others – *stay safe and alive.*

With this goal always in mind, horses are wired to live moment to moment. Humans (predators) on the other hand, have timelines and goals. We often live in the past or the future and are anything but present.   Horses don't have watches and they don't have calendars. There's not a problem with having an agenda, but a major disconnect can occur when we fail to consider these major differences between horses and humans.

Horses exhibit an enormous act of faith through their cooperation with us. If we want to take our barrel racing to the highest level possible, it makes sense to obtain as much *willing* cooperation from our horse as we can. Experiencing true unity when racing through the pattern, without delays or hesitation, is the stuff winning runs are made of. Whether it's a foal following its mother or a herd of horses moving in unison, horses are naturals at this. Humans – not so much. Often times, we sabotage the potential for this kind of unity with our horses, without even realizing it. The result is that our partner pulls away, either physically or mentally and the connection is damaged or lost.

What is it that fosters this kind of connection? The kind of unity that can carry a winning barrel racing team through when the chips are down? Once we get a grasp on just how huge the language barrier is between horses and humans, the next step comes in becoming *really* fluent at "speaking horse."

> 66 *If you are only a student of technique, then the options become very limited. On the other hand, when you are a student of the horse, the options are unlimited.* 99
>
> — Mark Rashid

Communicating in a way that horses easily understand does not come naturally to humans, so is something we must continually strive for and work on. When we don't, misunderstanding occurs. This lack of understanding on a large scale can result in the kicking, jerking, spanking, screaming, crying and cussing I mentioned in the introduction. This is extremely frustrating and can be potentially dangerous, but the horse is not the source of the problem – lack of communication skills in the human, IS.

Communication can be defined as two individuals, *both* sharing ideas and understanding each other; having a conversation. This doesn't mean they always agree, but they do their best to understand the others viewpoint. If you set out to teach your horse something without first developing excellent communication skills, it would be much like a foreigner that doesn't speak English trying to give you directions. There would be a lot of confusion and very little understanding going on. This lack of clarity is frustrating, stressful and discouraging to horses. When you commit to bettering your own communication skills, you take advantage of a huge opportunity to build your horse's confidence. Who doesn't want to do that?

When we start to build these communication skills ourselves, we also become better equipped to understand what horses are communicating to us. If we care about horses, and can "hear" how they feel, a new world of opportunity opens before us. Surprisingly, it's really not difficult to *make* a horse do what we ask.

Failure to Communicate

Obtaining *willing cooperation* is another game completely, and it all starts with understanding and meeting their needs.

The problem is, that of all the people who own horses, very few really understand what those needs are, and what is possible when they are met. Meeting each other's needs and responding to each other's requests becomes easy when both horse and rider are clear on *what those needs and requests are.* It's an incredible thing, and it all starts with learning their language.

Needs

All horses are wired with a deep, primary need for *safety*. Under the surface of even the most pushy, dominant horse is an instinctual need for quality leadership. This leadership goes to the individual who makes a request. This explains why briskly moving a horse's feet in different directions seems to have such a magical calming effect – it builds trust and respect. It's as if they can take a deep breath, lick their lips and say, "Whew, I'm so glad you have things under control, I can finally relax now!"

Building your horse's trust and respect takes time. It can be difficult to gain, and easy to lose. This is often the missing piece when a horse refuses to move his feet, won't stop moving his feet, is distracted, or even non-responsive. Fear is not always displayed in the form of the more obvious, outer fear witnessed when a horse spooks. A wide range of problems often exist because at a deep level, the horse's needs are not met. For any horse, this is good reason to be afraid – very afraid! Symptoms of fear will only disappear when the fear disappears – possible through quality leadership. When a horse's needs are adequately met, fear and insecurity (and the associated behaviors) dissolve.

When a horse perceives a lack of leadership, they will step into this roll themselves. Although many times weighing over 1,000 lbs., horses would really prefer us to be the brave one. They are natural followers. When you prove yourself as a skilled leader, you provide comfort for your horse and a relief from stress – you meet his greatest need. For an animal that is always on the lookout for his own safety, this is an *extremely valuable gift*.

❝ *The horse is so honest.... they live in the moment. And what they do, whether they need to protect themselves or whether they need to accept you really is directly relative to how you make them feel.* **❞**

— Buck Brannaman

It's not to say there won't be times when we ask them to step up and take on responsibilities in the partnership. The difference is that when we've done our part to meet their needs *first*, they'll be prepared, willing and confident in these moments.

When we see the world through a horse's eyes, we realize that behavior issues are not a matter of them being difficult, stupid, or stubborn. A true understanding of a horse's needs creates a greater level of compassion in the human. Be mindful however, that good horsemanship is not necessarily all gentle, all the time. Again, leadership goes to the one who makes a request. Never wishy-washy, a good leader is considerate but can actually seem quite bossy.

Under this primary need for safety are other needs that are also very important. Consider a horse that is laid back and calm, seemingly under any circumstances. This horse is likely to have a greater need for motivation, something to look forward to, a job to do, an understanding of a purpose behind all those circles. In addition to mental and emotional needs, are physical needs that also become much easier to meet, when we truly know what they are. As circumstances change, your horse's need for your reassurance, among other things, will change as well. Do your best to be aware and provide reminders of your leadership position even after a good relationship has been established.

Groundwork establishes leadership that transfers over under saddle.

This is where knowing your horse and being an excellent communicator comes in. Through watching and learning how a horse communicates with other horses, we can even further fine tune our methods of communication to resonate the most with each individual horse. When your horse has what he needs mentally, emotionally and physically, he feels relaxed and content, and will offer you freely and willingly what you ask. He is in harmony, in this herd of two, with you as the leader.

There is an old-school belief still lingering in parts of the barrel racing world that our horses will learn to be "tough" if we don't pamper them too much. The truth is that horses are more likely to build confidence in themselves and in their rider, when we set them up for success by meeting their needs to the best of our ability. In doing so, we're more likely to create positive experiences we can build upon.

Of course, in the process of developing a barrel horse, there will be moments when we ask them to stretch outside of their comfort zones. Growth and achievement is not possible without experiencing some level of discomfort. In these instances, ask yourself what you can do to make your horse's job easier, not harder. Throwing them into situations they aren't really ready for, to teach them to be "tough" or "deal with it" is actually more likely to contribute to the development of insecurities, in their environment, in themselves and in you. There *will* be circumstances that don't always allow you to provide the level of care and preparation that you would like. When you do so at every other opportunity, your horse is more likely to step up, and do his best for you in those less than ideal circumstances, with his confidence intact.

When we understand and start working through the language barrier with horses, on the other side are even more blocks that get in the way of building a relationship. A big one is our emotions. A challenging horse might evoke a response in us that has emotions behind it – like frustration and anger. When we feel these emotions, it's usually because we have run out of knowledge and lack the emotional fitness to deal with the problem without attaching emotion to it. A weak spot in our communication and leadership is brought to the surface, our horse makes it obvious.

As we've learned, horses live in the present, always doing what they feel is best at the moment to feel secure, with no concept of good or bad. A true horseman always gives a horse a chance to understand a subtle request first. When firmness is required, it can be delivered without anger or other emotions.

Horses are our mirror, what we get out of them is only as good as what we put in. We cannot teach horses what we don't first have ourselves. Before reaching high levels in horsemanship, we must get ourselves right on the inside. If we expect our horses to control their emotions, developing our own ability to do the same is a good place to start.

Developing our barrel horses, then is not as much about horse training as it is about self-development. This self-development route, however, isn't one all horse people are interested in taking. It's an incredible opportunity for growth but a responsibility to take seriously when we acquire an animal that relies on our understanding and leadership for its health and happiness.

Choices

If you barrel race long enough you will eventually notice a few horses and riders turning in fast times that have neither solid foundations nor true connections as partners. This is the exception more than the rule. Winning doesn't necessarily mean good horsemanship. Some barrel racers choose fear and intimidation to motivate their horses rather than commit to really understanding *why* horses behave as they do and how to effectively communicate with them.

When we develop good communication skills, we become someone our horse can trust and look to for safety and reassurance in times of uncertainty. If you're good at reading horses, you'll notice there are a lot of times like that. The better leader you are, the more comfort and security your horse feels. The misunderstandings are much less frequent and you both experience much more satisfaction and enjoyment together.

Because the way we get to our destination matters, we are not only concerned with what we can get our horse to do, but also how he feels about it. When you grab your halter, ask yourself, how can my horse win today? What's in it for him? When you make a request, does your horse answer "YES! Did I do it enough!?" If not – *why*? Ask yourself, whether your horse was loose in a parking lot, or if you were putting the first ride on a colt, if they became "lost," would the horse look to *you* for safety and reassurance or would he flee or explode in a blind panic? Think of the two of you as being on the same team. At the heart of every good relationship is a healthy balance of give and take, the relationship with your horse is no exception.

I wouldn't hesitate to match a horse with more talent that dreads running barrels to one that is less talented but full of enthusiasm and connection with their rider. When your horse *seeks* release rather than *avoids* pressure, when your horse offers performance based on *desire*, rather than *avoidance*, it can take your barrel racing to a whole new level. None of this can be injected like a vaccine or a pre-run cocktail. Understand your horse's mental, emotional and physical needs – and meet them. Give this gift to your horse, and he will *willingly* offer his best in return.

Some barrel racers will write this relationship off as not worth it or not possible. Some trainers have ten horses to ride in a day, and will say there simply isn't time to pay attention to each horse's needs and develop a deep connection with each of them. For some, the end goal is the priority, regardless of what is sacrificed to get there. There will always be consequences to the choices we make as we travel down the road to barrel racing success.

The truth is, it doesn't matter how well you ride, if you don't understand horses before you get on their back, if you can't cause a horse to release his opposition reflex and want to be with you, you're limiting your success in competition.

Truly understanding horses and becoming an effective communicator and skilled leader takes time, no doubt. Putting the horse first, in some instances, may take away profit from the bottom line. What building this relationship *adds*, however, is impossible to quantify and can take you and the horse to places in the competitive arena and in life you may have never thought possible.

I encourage you to make choices as you travel on your own individual path to barrel racing success that you can feel good about in the end. The sooner you understand *why* certain things work the way that they do, the sooner you'll figure out *how* to get the results that you want. Remember the *way* we go about all this *matters*, it matters the most to the horse.

So *how* can you start to develop a positive partnership with your horse?

- When it comes to building a relationship, it helps to start with the right horse. Sometimes it's clear when we start out, whether we want a horse with naturally high energy or low energy and a corresponding desire to move their feet. In many cases extroverted horses get along best with extroverted riders, with the same being true for those more on the introverted side. Don't necessarily rule out a prospect or lose hope with a horse you already have if they are your opposite. Although some horses may require more of a time investment to build a connection, these relationships can result in more growth in our horsemanship. It is also possible for an extroverted horse to have strengths that fill in the gaps for an introverted person and vice-versa. Through knowing yourself and knowing horses, you'll be better able to determine whether your differences will compliment each other, or grate against each other.

- There is much to be accomplished by doing nothing with your horse! Consider spending time simply *being* with your horse instead of always *doing*. When you do what he does, it develops rapport. It helps your horse realize that you don't always want something from him. Try including an extra ten minutes of time with no agenda before and/or after each ride. You might allow your horse to graze, give him a massage, or just sit quietly. Take advantage of opportunities to pause and study horses in their environments, become an avid student of the horse. Simply learning their habits and watching how they communicate with each other is a great way to become a better communicator yourself.

- Having a happy horse hinges directly on knowing what it is that makes your individual horse happy. All horses have a deep, primary, baseline need for safety. This can be provided through adequate communication and leadership. Beyond that, what are your horse's preferences? Does he prefer to lie down to nap? Does he like to run and play? Where are his favorite itchy spots? Is food a high priority for you horse? Relaxation time? Is he confident or insecure in certain areas? Does your horse seem to perform better in certain types of environments? Be mindful that any good relationship starts with two individuals spending time together and really getting to know what each other's needs are.

- When frustration and anger come up and you're tempted to channel it toward your horse, stop and look within. Realize that projected emotions are simply a reflection of what you have going on inside. Horses do not try to displease us on purpose – they are actually always looking for what they perceive as the path of least resistance based on their experiences. Instead of taking out frustration on your horse, work on adding to your toolbox of knowledge and skills. Your horse needs you to be the level-headed one, the one that can stay calm in any crisis. It's important to be firm when necessary, but do so in what I call "zombie mode," without emotion. Regardless of whether you're embarrassed, frustrated, angry, tired, cranky, etc. strive to set a good example of emotional fitness in your relationship.

- If your horse is communicating that he's interested in doing the opposite of what you would like, then make your idea, his idea. You might want your horse to stand still and be calm but he's full of energy. Put that energy to good use and work on dynamic, small, balanced circles with lots of change in direction. In no time standing still will seem like a good idea. Does your horse keep traveling crooked when you want to go straight? Start asking him for crazy circles and serpentines in all shapes and patterns, and soon your horse will be begging to go straight! This is using psychology rather than intimidation to get the results you want.

- Horses are very intuitive animals. They may not have proof of something being amiss, or spend time reasoning, but they can sense and feel things, sometimes before they actually happen. Intuition is part of their survival mechanism – they are very aware of their surroundings and sensitive to danger. We have the ability to tap into this power as well. If you just have a feeling that your horse needs a day off, or that you should check on him one more time, or have a feeling about something concerning his needs, by all means, follow your instincts and utilize this powerful source of knowledge.

- Seeing to your horse's physical needs is not only a way to invest in his health and longevity, but it can be part of facilitating a positive relationship as well. Be the person who feeds and waters your horse whenever possible. When your horse is comfortable – well rested, hydrated and doesn't have an empty stomach, and he sees that YOU are the one that delivers that comfort and meets his needs, he will not only perform better but it will contribute to the connection made.

" Feel is all the horse has to go on. "

– Bill Dorrance

Awareness and Feel

My glasses fogged up as my gelding and I stepped through the door into the heated arena. It was a blustery Wyoming winter day but a few miles from my home was a 50 degree paradise with perfect ground. It didn't matter how much cold and wind I endured to get there, two hours of precious riding time, free of snow, ice and numb fingers was always worth it. "Did you feel that!?" I didn't. "Yeah," I replied and nodded, to avoid being perceived as dense. My friend and mentor was pointing out an obvious (to her) problem in my horse's positioning as we worked the pattern. I didn't *feel it*, but at that point I realized that maybe I should have.

There is No Time That is Not Now

Always a very driven individual, my mind was incessantly spinning in the future, or projecting the past into the future. Accomplishing, doing, and checking items off the list made me feel good. While on a path of personal development I began to learn about the value of being present. I was resistant at first. For someone who sourced their worth from *doing*, simply *being* just didn't sound very appealing, or productive. In fact, deep down, it was more than a little scary.

Again, horses aren't concerned with being productive, that's something we bring into the picture. Horses are *always* living in the moment, being highly aware and sensitive to their environment is a way of life. So maybe there really was something to gain by being present.

For humans, being present is not so easy. As competitors, with our sights set on timelines and achieving goals, it becomes especially difficult and, unfortunately, this isn't the only thing that gets in the way. Society today puts a great deal of value on *doing*, which means our ability to be present in the moment is something most of us will need to continually work on.

Being fully present means the moment you grab a halter and step in your horse's direction, it's him and you and nothing else – no mental noise, no grocery lists, no dentist appointments, no what's for dinner, no phone calls or endless gabbing. Just you, and your horse – *in the moment.*

Being present is a prerequisite to awareness, the kind of true, heightened awareness that a rare-few real horsemen possess. Therefore, if our minds are in the future, or the in past, or in the grocery store, awareness is lost. When lost repeatedly, along with it goes our chance (and our horse's chance) to reach our greatest potential.

Eventually I became convinced that growth in my horsemanship, my personal life, *and* success running barrels, would depend on my ability to *"BE here now."* I realized in that quiet space, was something of far more value than a spinning mind could ever accomplish. In the moment, is where the magic happens.

There are different types of awareness that are crucial to good horsemanship. If we pay close enough attention and are present in the moment, our eyes will see things we never saw before, with a new awareness in our body we will physically feel that which we were unable to feel before. We will even notice an energetic awareness, intangible shifts in the air that we certainly feel, but cannot see or touch.

Before I understood the value of *being*, I was not fully utilizing my senses. True awareness requires getting out of our head and into our bodies. Major breakthroughs on the barrel pattern can occur through causing subtle changes in the form of foot placement, body position, weight shifts and more. These breakthroughs can only take place, IF we are aware enough to realize they are necessary.

> **66** *FEEL... that mysterious entity of communication which, once grasped and understood, somehow magically transforms horse and rider into a seemingly mythical unity of beauty, balance and harmony... opening secret doors of communication never before seen, heard or felt.* **99**
>
> – Michael Gonzalez

Awareness is useless without "feel." Feel is what puts awareness to good use, feel *is awareness in action.* Even though I didn't "feel it" that winter day in the barn, I have since revealed and continue to reveal a degree of feel that had been dormant throughout all my prior riding and competing experience. Many others are in the same boat. Of course, I had grown well beyond the kicking, pulling, and spanking ignorance of my early years. I had experienced some success in competition and was even starting colts, but looking back I see that I was clueless in the area of *feel.*

In circles of horse people, the word "feel" gets thrown around quite a bit, but few understand it and even fewer live it. Although nearly impossible to teach, I believe that it's possible and worthwhile to harness the power of words, metaphors and simulations in effort to demystify the concept of feel. In the end, however, "feel" is really something that must be experienced to be fully appreciated and understood.

A great metaphor to describe feel involves a couple learning to dance. In the beginning the dance instructor describes the movements, and all the many subtleties of correct body posture.

Initially both students are stiff and there is some pushing and pulling. In time, they no longer have to look at their feet but might step on each other now and then. Eventually they learn to glide smoothly around the dance floor, without even having to think about how to hold their bodies and place their feet.

A moment arrives when rather than sticking to a choreographed pattern, they are moving with *feel*. The male leads the female freely and effortlessly, they stare into each other's eyes  and twirl as each partner remains in their space regardless of change in direction. They consistently meet each other in their movement, one always slightly leading, the other always right there with them, moving together in perfect harmony. They have learned to let go, and just *feel*.

Some instructors teach ballroom dancing first by requiring partners to learn the moves standing side by side, facing the same direction. When this is accomplished they practice the moves with timing when facing each other. Eventually they do the same with their bodies connected and only when this is perfect, do they finally connect their arms.

This teaching method demonstrates what would be an ideal way to learn to ride with awareness, feel and timing. We must learn how to maintain our own balance and posture (without pushing and pulling) independently of each other first, before anything beautiful can be created together.

The most basic component of feel is the application and release of pressure, which is a main line of communication in the horse world. More specifically, feel is not so much direct pressure as implied pressure. Like the two dancers maintaining an equal cushion of space between each other as they move around the dance floor, a horse and rider also *meet each other* by keeping space. A horse responds and yields as pressure is coming and a rider flows with the movement of a horse, filling any excess void and constantly maintaining rhythm, harmony and togetherness.

Feel is more than something in our hands when holding the reins in the saddle. We can use heightened sensitivity and energetic awareness in our entire bodies, all of our senses, to feel of our horse at any time.

Without feel, movement is mechanical, insensitive and thought out in our head. In the beginning, the dancer's movements are jerky and uncoordinated. Over time, with conscious understanding and effort, they develop better sensitivity and awareness of each other.

Riders that have feel are present in the moment. They have a bodily awareness that allows them to notice subtle changes in their horse's position and demeanor. Not only do they notice subtle signs of resistance or yielding, they understand what caused it, what to do about it and when, to create the result they are looking for.

❝ *As we know, thinking ahead is the key to good horsemanship. If the horse goes to move off and we don't feel it until he takes a step, we are generally creating a brace if we take a square hold to stop him. Things can be much softer when we sense movement and get there early.* ❞

— Jan Leitschuh

The anticipation of the application and release of pressure may be the foundation of feel, but it's much more than that. A dancer or a rider with feel is also a master of timing. If the male dancer started to step backwards just as the woman was bringing her feet back down to contact the floor, it would be very difficult for the woman to follow his feel. If he stepped back just as she was beginning to take her next step, following his lead would be much easier.

The Time Has Come

Timing is what brings results to our feel. With proper timing, we set our horses up to perform maneuvers with greater ease and understanding, which accelerates learning. When you ride with timing and feel, you will *ask less* and *get more*.

Anyone can apply pressure, whether it be with a rein, with their body, or simply their energy, even from a distance. Knowing the exact fraction of a second to release the pressure requires good timing. Pulling and kicking without feel and timing sets a horse up for discouragement. Appropriate firmness and timing will bring out the best in

Timing is everything.

each horse. Good timing is a characteristic of feel, and when we grasp these concepts we are on our way to becoming better communicators with horses.

So what does "feel" *look* like?

With feel, a rider knows when a trotting horse will be loping on the next stride. A person with feel will influence feet as they are just coming off the ground, making stops, turns and acceleration easy and almost effortless for the horse. With feel, a rider moves their hands, seat and body with the horse's movement, instead of inconsiderately bumping the horse's mouth or sides. A person operating with feel knows when a horse is adequately warmed up or needs more preparation. With feel, a rider can confidently correct a horse that is out of position in the moment, whether in slow work or even in a run. In addition to being aware of footfall, a rider with feel can sense subtle shifts in weight and will time their requests based on this for maximum results. A rider with feel will apply pressure to a horse hesitant to go forward at the specific moment that is most likely to create the desired response. With feel, a person knows the exact moment to step back or turn to influence a horse in the round pen. A rider with feel knows when to apply more pressure and when to just get out of the way and wait for the horse to seek release and discover the desired response in their own time. With feel, a rider is better able to stay *with* their horse and in unison, no matter how fast or erratic the movement. A rider with feel senses and addresses potential problems before they even develop and heads them off at the pass.

Whether doing ground work or blasting down the alley, a horse and rider with feel can achieve harmony and togetherness under all circumstances. Once we find feel and start to build on it, we get along better with horses and experience much less resistance. Problems and obstacles seem to melt away while accelerated progress and success takes their place.

Myth vs. Fact

When it comes to feel, don't be discouraged by the common belief that some people are just "born with it," and some not. We ALL have feel, some of us just lose touch and must rediscover the ability. As we grow and experience life, blocks develop that get in the way of our feel. If we are dedicated students, we can journey "backward" and remove those blocks to the natural feel we are all born with. Remember, that although hours in the saddle, books, clinics and DVD's play their part, the "feel" you seek from outside sources, *already exists within you.*

66 *Above all, let us begin to feel! The ability to feel is a gift from God to each one of us. Let us begin to feel ourselves and understand our horses.* 99

– Klaus Ferdinand Hempfling

I hope that my perception and description of awareness and feel will provide barrel racers with clarity in an area that is often otherwise grey. Below I've included some additional metaphors, simulations and other tools that have made a great impact on my journey to riding and living with feel.

- To get out of your head and into your body, imagine riding your horse with your head chopped off! Sounds gruesome, yes, but it can open up an entirely new concept of what it means to be present in your body. If you didn't have a head or didn't even have eyes to see, would you be more aware of your body and conscious of what you are doing with it as you are riding?

- To improve your timing, be mindful of your horse's entire body. As you ride, practice counting when each foot either lifts or lands on the ground. Do this starting at a walk, then trot and lope. Initially, you may need to lean over and see which foot is doing what, in order to make the connection between what is really happening and how it feels. Learn how to trot on the correct diagonal and then make it your goal to consistently start rising and sitting on the correct one as you transition into a trot. (For more on diagonals see the *Rider Responsibilities* chapter.) For every change in gait or direction, be aware of the moment you ask and what the feet are doing at that split second. Experiment with timing and look for results that feel instant and effortless.

- There may be times when a horse does not seem to seek your release. This could occur for a variety of reasons, and it's our responsibility to understand why and inspire them to do so. For a horse that lacks a proper educational foundation, better timing of the application and release of pressure may solve the problem. A horse may also have a physical problem that makes it difficult for them to follow through. If you've had a habit of riding without feel, your horse may simply lose interest in meeting you halfway. Luckily, horses are very forgiving. It's never too late to start feeling of your horse, and inspiring him to feel of you.

- If you seem to be getting a grasp of what feel is, you may still be unsure of the subtleties of what is correct vs. incorrect when training or riding a barrel horse. Because I spent so many years unaware, I wasn't sensitive enough to truly observe, remember and compare what kind of movement got what result. To develop my understanding I rode with accomplished horseman and barrel racers and asked them to watch me and comment as I rode. Although I had a new level of awareness, I still wasn't confident that what I was feeling was correct. They would tell me the exact moments when they could see that my horse and I had collection or the perfect body position. I made a point to memorize those feelings in my body for future reference.

- There are numerous blocks that may get in the way of a rider experiencing feel. One is lack of balance in the saddle. Feel comes more naturally when we are not bracing on the reins or stirrups. (This is also covered in more detail in the *Rider Responsibilities* chapter.)

- To better understand the concept of feel, balance the end of a broom handle on your finger so that the bristled end is up in the air. It may tip from side to side and you must anticipate and meet that movement in order to keep it from falling. Meet your horse's movement and expect him to meet yours in a similar way. Some other activities that require feel are removing the seeds from a pomegranate, driving a stick shift, or spreading peanut butter on soft bread. In all these examples, the application and release of pressure in just the right way, and at just the right time, is critical.

66 *Few things can help an individual more than to place responsibility on him, and to let them know that you trust him.* 99

— Booker T. Washington

Horse Positioning

There is a psychological theory that describes four stages of learning. It suggests that when learning a new skill, individuals initially don't know what they don't know, or are unconsciously incompetent. As they recognize this, they start to acquire a skill and become conscious of their incompetence in a certain area. The third stage is conscious competence, which is when an individual understands and can perform a skill, but it requires concentration. Finally the fourth stage is unconscious competence. In this stage skills have become highly developed and become second nature, requiring little thought. As so many do, I spent years in the unconsciously incompetent stage, where the ignorance outweighed the bliss by a long shot.

As I finally started to develop awareness, I more easily recognized my blind spots and began to know there was a lot that I did not know. With a new sense of feel and timing, there were light bulbs coming on all over the place, especially when it came to noticing and influencing the way my horse was using his body. If barrel races are won and lost by a tiny fractions of a second, then it's no surprise that subtle changes, such as shifts of weight imperceptible to the eye, or changes in foot placement by margins as narrow as an inch, can be the difference between first place and second. If we compile all the subtle improvements that can be made in our horse's posture and positioning, it can yield big returns in the form of precious time shaved off the clock.

When a horse is using his body in an efficient way, it's as if he has created an open channel of energy to move easily, powerfully and quickly around the barrels. Below are some examples describing less than ideal body position, where this free flow of energy is blocked.

- A horse places weight on his front end and disengages the hind end, taking away power necessary to leave the turn with quickness and impulsion.

- The undesirable placement of a horse's feet on the path to the first barrel makes it impossible to position his body for an efficient turn when he gets there.

- A horse prepares for a turn too soon and leans extremely to the inside, which takes away balance and creates risk of falling.

- A horse dives into a turn stiffly with his rib cage toward the barrel, increasing the chances of tipping, and requiring the horse to take extra steps as he leaves the turn.

Horses performing with more extreme examples of the issues mentioned above are usually easy to recognize. Often times however, body position problems are subtle and riders lack the awareness to notice them and the skills to address them. Gone unnoticed, incorrect body position will create delays in a run and prevent a horse from clocking the fast times they are actually capable of.

Do you know exactly where your horse's feet are?

If we were to visualize our horse running through a giant tube that flexed around the barrel pattern like a straw, we could better understand how good positioning can create efficiency and poor positioning can cause time consuming delays.

Think of an entire barrel run taking place inside that large straw. A horse with good positioning will follow curves around the barrels like the curve in a straw that flexes at the top, allowing your favorite beverage to change direction but flow freely through it. A horse with poor positioning will come into a turn and hit a kink in the straw (like a kink in a hose) instead of an open, arcing bend that allows free forward movement. These kinks can appear at some barrels and not others, at times the kinks are big and *really* block the flow of energy and other times they are smaller, still hindering the horse, but to a lesser degree. Sometimes the straw is even pinched off in the straight away between barrels. Rider error can also cause kinks in the straw. In most cases the horse can make their way through these kinks, but at a much slower pace than if there were no blockages.

The first step in determining if your horse is operating at full capacity is to develop an ample dose of awareness and feel as discussed in the previous chapter. Until you are confident in this area, employ the help of someone who possesses a greater level of awareness and feel. Ask them to watch and describe what they see as you ride. As awareness develops, every ride will provide new insights.

Simple trial and error will allow you to develop confidence in knowing whether what you're feeling is correct or needs improvement. Ask yourself, does it feel easy? Does it feel light? Does it feel fast? Does it feel smooth? As each little light bulb comes on, embody and memorize what you feel as you make connections between specific positioning adjustments and the positive results you achieve.

Free & Easy

You might wonder why horses don't do more on their own to maneuver the pattern efficiently. Why would they have tendencies to run in a way that was not smooth and efficient?

The answer to that comes in considering several factors. The first one being that the horse may not have been properly taught how to use his body efficiently with a rider on his back when away from the pattern, so naturally issues occur on the barrels. Secondly, as riders, we are often times the actual reason they tend to position their bodies incorrectly. If we are imbalanced in our own bodies, override, or have poor timing, we will create kinks in the straw.

In addition, we would also be wise to again consider the differences between horses and humans. Horses eventually realize that barrel racing is an activity in which speed is involved, yes, but not necessarily that it's a race, a competition. Horses are wired to do what seems the most comfortable and logical *in the moment.* Sometimes contorting their bodies to avoid insensitive cues from their rider makes sense. Sometimes an unconscious rider actually teaches their horse to position themselves improperly. Ill fitting equipment can cause a horse to use their bodies inefficiently. Some horses might feel as though it's just easier to turn when they over prepare and lean to the inside.

What horses (and riders) don't often realize, until perhaps they've fallen down during a run, is that incorrect positioning and imbalanced movement not only creates delays, it can put them at more risk for injury. It's up to us to help our horses learn the subtleties of correct body position in order to maneuver the pattern in the most efficient and safest way possible. It's also our responsibility to stay out of their way, to make sure we, as riders, are not creating blocks in the barrel racing straw.

66 *With anything there is to do with horses, there are about a hundred different ways to get it done. Maybe 70 or 75 of those ways will work... but maybe only 10, or 15, of those ways are a good deal for the horse.* 99

— Unknown

When taking on this responsibility for the horse, there is a fine balance to achieve. It's important that we not become too rigid in dictating our horse's method for getting around the barrel pattern. We have to make the call when it comes to determining whether their individual tendencies are acceptable or if they will create delays. With some horses, it's a matter of not allowing body position tendencies to become too extreme. For example, many successful horses have a front-endy style in which they carry the majority of their weight on their front end in a turn. As long as they are able to keep forward motion, their preferred style may very well be fast and not cause a kink in the flow of energy.

Again this is where awareness and feel come in. Have a base understanding of what is typically correct versus incorrect and then ask yourself, - "does my horse's positioning cause a delay in our runs or a potential safety issue?" Is there a potential for a kink to develop in the future that will require my extra awareness as we progress? Be confident and trust your ability to make adjustments to your horse's body position as necessary. At the same time, remain flexible, keep an open mind, and listen to your horse.

Isolate & Separate

None of the topics in this book alone are the missing link to becoming a winning barrel racer. As I'm sure you're seeing, all the areas discussed are intricately connected and depend upon one another. So it should be no surprise that to successfully influence a horse's body position requires a solid educational foundation, also described in a previous chapter. With this foundation in place, a rider is able to move parts of a horse's body anywhere, and at any time. This means that we should be able to use our feel to imply and apply pressure and cause their body parts to either move up, down, right, left, forward or back under any circumstances.

To get a real feel for what I mean, turn your own head to the left then to the right as far as you can. Then facing forward, bring your chin all the way down, then stretch your head back as far as possible. Bring your head back to a natural position then stretch your neck toward the ceiling then compress it, bringing your chin lower without actually tipping your head forward. Go through all these movements, separating parts of your body like your neck shoulders, torso, hips and legs. Although different from a horse's body, it's surprising to realize just how much movement is possible when we isolate each individual area in our own bodies.

As we know, horses must understand how to yield from pressure, and be willing to yield, in all areas of their body, in order to learn proper positioning. Although this subject is covered in greater detail in the *Quality of Movement* chapter, the many, many details involved in how to accomplish this, again, go beyond the scope of this book.

Learning to yeild from leg pressure

I will remind you though that the basic stages for gaining control of a horse's body start with the application and release of pressure. When pressure and release are introduced to a horse on the ground first, understanding transfers over under saddle, making it easier for a horse to respond to similar requests made when on their back. We teach a horse to move their body parts by first offering a steady or rhythmic feel and waiting for them to seek the release, with good timing the right choice is rewarded instantly.

There will be moments when it's necessary to increase the application of pressure. However, because the lightness of a horse's response is based on the lightness in which we make our request, a rider with feel always gives the horse a chance to respond to light pressure first. A horse's understanding of yielding their body parts to our pressure begins at a standstill, starting with basic lateral flexion, side passing, etc. As they advance, more body parts are involved as well as gaits.

Recombine & Connect

As you sink more deeply into developing your awareness and horsemanship skills, you'll begin to see more and more connections everywhere. How we handle our horses on the ground really does transfer over under saddle. And what we do away from the barrels influences what happens on the barrel pattern.

When this light bulb comes on, it's quite a gift because this means that we can perform drills, exercises and make corrections away from the barrel pattern, keeping the barrel pattern a positive learning environment for the horse. Without awareness on your side, you're unlikely to see and take advantage of this connection.

If your horse tends to lean to the inside in a turn, with awareness you'd notice that he leans in his circles in general. A horse that doesn't stay on track while working the pattern will also waver off path when asked to take responsibility for traveling in straight lines away from the pattern. Be *aware* and look for ways in which the issues your horse has on the barrels show up elsewhere.

A great barrel horse loves running barrels. Be committed to keeping that spark alive by taking advantage of the ability to influence what happens on the barrels by schooling and making corrections away from the pattern.

> **66** *You allow a horse to make mistakes, the horse will learn from mistakes no different than the human. But you can't get him to where he dreads making mistakes for fear of what's going to happen after he does.* **99**

— Buck Brannaman

Blaze Your Own Trail

We all follow the same basic cloverleaf trail around the barrels, but the variations of the path we train our horses feet to follow varies greatly. Many successful barrel horse trainers develop their own idea of exactly where those feet should fall and they typically don't vary far off that path when training different horses.

Years ago, making a large pocket while approaching the turn was standard practice. When barrel racers started to apply the "science of speed" to barrel racing, we realized that the fastest way between two points was a straight line, so for the most part, the pocket idea went out the window. Some barrel racers believe in keeping an equal distance around the barrels. Some still allow a little more room when coming in the turn as opposed to leaving. Some barrel racers prefer a little extra room on the back side of a turn. There are trainers that like a square turn, and others keep the turns very round. Some riders train their horses to follow a certain path in slow work and another path with speed. Some believe that adjustments should be made to accommodate each horse.

Although I have identified a specific path that I prefer *my* horse's feet to fall around the barrel pattern, I am not in a position to declare a certain way as right or wrong because behind each successful barrel horse is a slightly differing path. What I do recommend is finding a route around the barrels that makes sense and resonates with you and sticking to it. Of course if you realize over time that something isn't working, don't hesitate to change it. Be mindful along the way that one of the horse's greatest needs in life is for consistency. Don't allow extra room on the backside of the barrel when doing slow work one day, and make a big pocket the next.

When a horse knows the exact placement of his feet on the pattern will never change, it builds confidence. Lack of consistency will cause a horse to hesitate and become unsure of himself. Do your best to be specific without being critical and remember that consistency leads to confidence.

Horse Responsibilities

Once proper body position is achieved when working the pattern, many barrel racers run into trouble trying to maintain it. Let's go back to our metaphor involving the two dancers; if the female was not playing a physically and mentally active part in the dance, it would require the male to over compensate. In a true partnership, both parties have responsibilities to uphold.

This means that when we ask our horse to trot, he keeps trotting until given instructions otherwise. This means that if we ask our horses to circle and our body position suggests that he stays in that circle, he doesn't drift off path. This means, that although we must stay mentally focused on where we are going and visualize what we want, we must not *hold* our horses in position through the over use of our hands and legs.

It's critical that horses develop responsibility for carrying themselves correctly with little guidance. When the time comes to add speed, a horse that is over-dependent on his rider will be unable to efficiently maneuver that pattern without a lot of perfectly timed assistance, which can be difficult if not impossible, and will cause delays in a run for even the most advanced rider.

The ultimate barrel horse is one that is confident and prepared enough to make his own good choices, but does not completely take over. Ideally, we are ever so slightly in the lead and when we present a feel, our horse takes responsibility to meet us. If we do our part, not much in the way of corrections will be required. At the same time, a winning barrel horse is willing to accept help or correction from a rider without resistance in those situations when it becomes necessary.

This doesn't happen by magic, we must do our part to prepare, educate, develop and trust our horse before they will be successful in taking on the responsibility to maintain their body position. This means that we must be striving toward this delicate balance at all times, whether on the ground, under saddle, on the barrel pattern or away from it. When we trust a horse, we are setting a positive intention. As we meet a horse's needs and teach him to take responsibility and be responsive to us, he becomes self-assured, ready to perform with confidence, yet willing to follow our slightest suggestion. By fostering independence in our horses on the pattern, we are building their confidence and allowing them to live up to their highest potential, and making it easier on us as riders in the process.

When it comes to maintaining correct body position, again there are numerous potential causes for blockages in the free flow of energy around the barrel pattern. (Several more will be discussed in greater detail in the following chapter on *Rider Responsibilities*.)

Barrel races are won and lost, and lives are even changed by differences in times down to the thousandths of a second. Very subtle positioning adjustments can change everything. The details matter. When we develop the ability to notice positioning issues and make necessary adjustments, we are setting ourselves up to maneuver the barrel pattern as quickly and as efficiently possible.

66 *The horse can't run faster than I can ride him.* **99**

– Ray Hunt

Rider Responsibilities

I titled this chapter *Rider Responsibilities* because I feel as though it's important to do our best to keep our horses healthy and happy. Good riding is part of that. When a problem comes up, we must ask ourselves, "What have I done to cause this?" Blame is so commonly placed on the horse, when poor riding is often the cause of tipped barrels, lack of engagement in the hind end, body soreness, cross firing and more. When we focus on improving ourselves, we open a door to our horse's greatest potential in the process.

So what constitutes a good rider in barrel racing anyway? We might believe if we can lope circles, perform roll backs, and make a high speed run without major day-lighting in the saddle that we are accomplished riders. Some might assume that anyone who has been riding since they were old enough to walk is automatically a good rider.

Many have the misconception that good riders look a certain way, they have an ability to maintain a certain body position. If barrel racers aren't judged on their form, do the subtleties of our body position really matter anyway? If we were to ask the ultimate judge, our horse, the answer would be a resounding YES!

When someone at the barrel race says "She can really ride!" it may mean that person has an ample dose of balance, timing, fluidity & feel that is necessary to be *one* with a horse during a run. Some of us may have taken riding lessons in the past, or have experience showing in 4-H, in which we were taught proper position of our bodies. Having this proper posture in the warm-up pen is not necessarily an indication of being one with our horse. We may have the look, but what we really want is the *feel* – and under all circumstances. Whether we have this or not becomes more obvious in a high speed event like barrel racing. Great riders communicate to their horse with feel and timing, which creates a *response* rather than *reaction* in a run. They are balanced and fluid in their body, appearing to move "with" versus "on" their horse.

A not so advanced rider might cue their horse too soon or too late (lack of timing), they might tense up and brace in the stirrups (lack of fluidity), lean one way or another (lack of balance) or make over exaggerated movements and jerk or pull their horse through a turn (lack of feel), as they try to make up for the mistakes created by an absence of one or more of the elements mentioned above – timing, fluidity, balance and feel!

66 *How can our horses respond to a whisper when we are always screaming at them?* 99

— Walter Zettl

Without all of these crucial elements that make up good riding, we make our horse's job much more difficult. As we compensate in our bodies for what we lack, our horse also compensates in his body, leading to soreness. As a good rider, we can enhance our horse's movement rather than get in the way of it. In gratitude for their service to us, the least we can do is put effort into becoming a better rider and make carrying us as easy, comfortable and stress-free as possible.

Balance

Previous chapters of this book have increased our understanding and appreciation for timing and feel, the time has come to study the meaning and effects of balance and fluidity.

Until we develop true balance on our horse, our bodies will always hold tension and seek ways to feel secure. Saddles and reins are often used unconsciously as a crutch, something for our bodies to brace against and counteract our lack of balance. Poor timing is often the result of poor balance. When a horse and rider get out of sync in a run, the horse must shift his own body so the rider can "catch up." When we are not one with our horse and properly balanced, as in the case of a rider that leans, stiffens or uses too much or too little rein, we become "extra baggage" and are dramatically interfering with our horse's ability to use their own bodies in an efficient (and fast) way. You may have carried tension in your body so long without realizing it, that it's hard to detect; however, your horse (and the clock) knows the truth! When we are balanced we can do a better job of gently guiding our horse in a run, only doing what is necessary – no more and no less. When we are free and supple, less "pull" is required, and when we can sit squarely and securely, everything becomes much easier for the horse – they can do their job better, with more ease and freedom of movement.

❝ *When you ride a horse, balance comes, not from freezing your legs to the saddle, but from learning to float with the movement of the horse as you ride. Each step is a dance, the rider's dance as well as the dance of the horse.* **❞**

— Chogyam Trungpa Rinpoche

An issue with my own balance came to light a few years ago as I experimented with a simple exercise that involved trotting in small circles without stirrups. As I rode a long strided trot and made a small circle to the right, with every stride I slipped an inch further to the outside of my saddle, soon I was scratching my fingernails to scramble back up! Without my left stirrup to brace in, I was almost a goner. I discovered a severe habit of bracing in my left stirrup – it was my body's way of compensating for a lack of balance. This explained why my saddle would shift and require me to step hard to the other side to straighten it. Compensation can also show up in the form of erratic hand movements, among other things. Our ability to ride our horses in a way that helps rather than hinders them hinges directly on having good balance.

Instead of becoming depressed by the realization of my shortcomings as a rider, I was excited to have found something I *knew* had been blocking my success. I focused on my riding and rode often without stirrups or bareback. Without anything to brace against, I was forced to better develop my independent seat and find that sweet spot where our centers of gravity meet and we achieve oneness. I also gained a better understanding of another key ingredient to harmony when riding, that of fluidity.

Fluidity

Developing fluidity, just as the word implies, means moving in a way that is fluid versus stiff or rigid. Fluidity is accomplished by loosening up our bodies and using all our joints. Most riders have a tendency to overuse certain body parts and underuse others. For example a rider might have flexibility and suppleness in their lower back but stiffness in their knees or shoulders. As herd animals, horses have a natural ability to move smoothly in harmony with others. The movement we want to model would be similar to that of a school of fish. When they go, we go, when they slow, we slow. When we're in harmony with fluidity, regardless of how fast or erratic our horse's movement, we stay with them. This means that a good rider will never experience a runaway, because they can always ride as fast as any horse can run!

Mirror, Mirror

Barrel racers don't often realize how powerful the position of a rider's body can be when it comes to helping horses perform at their optimum level. Remember that horses very easily take on the energy of their environment. This is how they have evolved over millions of years, by being very aware and doing what others do around them to stay safe. They have a natural tendency to do in their body what we do in ours. We hold the power to help our horse's position their own bodies through properly positioning our own.

This might mean building energy in your body to bring some life into your horse's steps. It might mean becoming quiet and calm so as to soothe a nervous horse. It will mean picking up your own shoulder or bending in your own ribcage if this is what you want in your horse. If you want your horse to keep his forward momentum

in a turn, pump your seat energetically with each stride. Become fluid and free in your own body, watch as your horse releases tension and does the same. If you want your horse to lope slower, slow down the rocking motion of your seat.

Any areas where you lack flexibility and suppleness are areas your horse will also. To limit yourself to only using your hands and legs to communicate with your horse, or to be unaware of your own improper positioning creates a huge handicap. Horses really are our mirror, in more ways than one. Experiment with these concepts and prepare to see positive results as you become empowered with a new way to enhance your horse's ability to position and move his body.

Have you ever beat yourself up mentally for not riding as well in a run as you thought you should have, not remembering to do "this or that" when your horse needed guidance? The truth is that great riders do not rely on *thinking* their way through a run. Through developing an advanced degree of balance, timing, fluidity & feel, excellent riding becomes second nature. This is where stage four of learning, or conscious competence occurs. Great barrel racers don't *make* a horse work, they do their homework, set the horse up to succeed and then *allow* a horse to perform without getting in his way, which is truly a win for both horse and rider.

Becoming a great rider is yet another way in which we can meet our horse's needs. We can provide comfort and relief of stress through our commitment to improving ourselves. Our horses will be healthier, happier and will perform better as a result. Because so much focus is placed on horses, developing riding ability specifically for barrel racing is somewhat of a grey area. Success is found in the details. I've included some tips below for bettering your riding that have proven to be extremely helpful on my own journey:

- If you think your balance is already above average, as a test – kick your feet free of the stirrups and long trot the barrel pattern. You may be surprised by the lack of security you feel! Focus on circles! Balance issues will really show up when long trotting circles, the smaller they are the more the "holes" in our riding are amplified! As you're circling, also avoid the temptation to allow yourself or your horse to lean too much to the inside. Visualize yourself and your horse being squarely balanced with equal weight distribution on each side.

- To improve balance, ride bareback for 30 to 60 minutes at least once a week (try to keep your bareback riding sessions short to avoid creating soreness in your horse due to the lack of weight distribution). Simply losing the saddle requires that we automatically become more relaxed, fluid and in time with our horse. Reason being, if you were too stiff – you'd be on the ground! Do everything bareback that you would do otherwise, but at your own comfort level. Be very aware and get a feel for how good your balance really is. Avoid the temptation to lean too far forward or use your legs to grip. Remember to stay relaxed and fluid in your joints and move with your horse's movement, even exaggerating your movement. Take this opportunity to really FEEL your horse under you, which foot falls and when, which muscles are engaged, etc.

- Commit to posting on the correct diagonal at all times. Especially important in a turn, posting on the correct diagonal is critical to the balance and conditioning of you and your horse. A trot is a two beat diagonal gait, the feet hit the ground in diagonal pairs. When your seat rises as the outside front foot/inside back foot comes forward and lowers when they go back ("rise and fall with the front leg on the wall"), you are lifting up and lightening some of the load on the inside where the horse will tend to weight himself more. You also can better encourage your horse to reach deep under himself with the inside hind leg when you are on the correct diagonal. Posting on the correct diagonal will help in developing you and your horse's muscles symmetrically. Learn to feel the correct diagonal when you transition into a trot, rather than sitting two beats to get on the correct diagonal after you are already trotting. In time, posting on the correct diagonal becomes something you do without conscious thought.

- If your horse is not taking an active role in your partnership, this will make it difficult for you to ride properly. It is our responsibility to make sure he understands his responsibilities. Having to consistently micro-manage a horse that is extremely lazy or overly active and distracted will require that you revisit some basics to get on the same page. Ensure that your horse has a solid educational foundation, and do your part to develop your own communication skills and provide good quality leadership. Don't hesitate to employ a professional to assist with this process. Once your horse better understands what is expected, and is a willing partner, it is then possible to work on developing more refinement as a rider.

- In general, barrel racers tend to have a habit of leaning too far forward. This actually interferes with our horse's ability to elevate their front end and engage their hind end properly. In addition, be careful that you're not placing your saddle too far forward which also hinders free movement of the shoulders. Both of these issues can be the cause for a kink in the barrel racing straw. To encourage free flowing, forward movement, raise your chin, lift and open your own upper body and visualize your horse elevating his front end as he moves.

- Use your new found awareness and feel to be aware of your horse's whole body, especially the hind end. We may not always be able to see what is behind us, but remember there is a lot of horse back there that must also be taken into consideration. Use your body to influence and ride your whole horse, being aware of the hind end and drive your horse forward with your own seat if necessary. Rather than hurry a turn, remember that the hind end must be allowed to finish, and get in a balanced position for a powerful departure.

- Ride blindfolded or with your eyes closed (on a quiet, familiar horse) in a small arena or round pen. Practice going where the horse goes with fluidity rather than resistance. Visualize any tension melting away and become very fluid in your joints. Walk, trot and lope without holding the reins, zig and zag, go and slow – together. Ride with *feel*, and heightened awareness, go *with* your horse's every move. Do you think you could stay *with* your horse even if he moved quickly or erratically? This practice of surrendering control can really bring to light how resistant and out of sync we are. Consider wearing knee guards for this exercise if you think your horse might travel too close to the fence.

- Get on your hands and knees for a couple of very eye opening simulations. Lower your waist to create a hollow, concave back. Try crawling forward while bringing your legs as far underneath you as possible. Now try this again with your back lifted and rounded. This simulation demonstrates just how difficult quality movement can become with our bodies in less than ideal position. Next, while still on your hands and knees, try turning a sharp circle on all fours with your rib cage bent toward the inside of the turn. Try the circle again with your mid-section shaped like the barrel; feel a difference? Take this new awareness with you when you ride and do your part to help rather than hinder your horse's ability to properly position his own body.

- It doesn't feel quite right to expect from others what we are unwilling to do ourselves. We put a lot of time and effort into getting our horses fit, strong and flexible and because they are our mirror, it's wise to develop a fitness program for ourselves that will specifically benefit us as riders. Consider playing volleyball, racquetball, tennis or any other sport that requires hand/eye coordination. Participate in a dance fitness or zumba class that will improve your timing. Enroll in a Yoga class to increase your flexibility or get a Pilates DVD to work out at home and increase your core strength. If you aren't able to make it into town regularly, there are Yoga, Pilates and other fitness programs available on DVDs that were developed just for equestrians. Between riding, cleaning pens and lugging hay bales, you may get plenty of activity in; on those days when you aren't as active, participate in one of the above mentioned activities or just do some kind of movement that you enjoy and that feels good. Exercise is vital to being at our best, not just physically but mentally and emotionally as well. Becoming fit, strong and flexible will improve your riding. Find a routine that works for you, it can and should be enjoyable, not torturous.

• Many riders don't know how poorly they feel because they've never made self-care a priority. Adequate sleep, as well as proper diet and exercise allows our mind and body to react more quickly, giving us an edge in competition. In addition, we'll also experience increased energy, and greater emotional well-being. Eating well starts with knowing what's in our food, and then determining what to eat in moderation and which foods are okay to indulge in. Try eating six smaller meals throughout the day rather than three large meals to avoid crashes in blood sugar levels that lead to fatigue and binging. Pay close attention to what makes you feel good. Prepare healthy foods in advance to avoid temptation to grab less healthy options when time is short. Dehydration can cause headaches and fatigue, drinking adequate water helps your body operate as efficiently as possible. Experiment with cutting out dairy or lowering sugar or carbohydrate intake. Make it your goal to exercise and eat well for two weeks, just as a trial period. Be very aware of how you FEEL, mentally and physically. If you can do this, you'll likely be convinced that those habits are worth carrying out full time.

• A big mental block that gets in the way of good riding is subconscious fear. Even if we don't feel afraid on the surface, it's not uncommon for deep, subconscious fears to exist. Perhaps we've had one or several negative experiences when riding. Sometimes these fears are parallel to fears in our personal life, such as fear of losing control, fear of making a mistake or fear of what other people think. These are fears that we usually don't even realize we have. These subconscious fears can paralyze progress in our horsemanship and in the barrel racing arena. Consider how your horse might be influenced by these fears that could be causing you to subtly hesitate or hold back, and interfere with your feel and timing. In the case of a barrel racer that has done everything under the sun to improve, with minimal results, subconscious fear may be to blame. There is hope for overcoming these mental blocks and they will be discussed in the *Inner Game* chapter.

We are what we repeatedly do. Excellence then, is not an act, but a habit.

— Aristotle

Quality of Movement

When it comes to achieving greatness in any area, meaningless action is not enough – it is implementation that really matters. We can be busy doing things with our horse, but that doesn't mean we'll be effective. We must realize where our weaknesses are and have the driving desire to do *something* about it that will create results. We don't always know initially if changes we implement will create a positive difference; yet, when it comes to the way in which our horses move, there is much we can do to put the odds more in our favor.

In a previous chapter, we talked about the paths we train our horse's feet to follow on the barrels, and how that can vary, even between the world's most successful barrel horses. Although the differences are many, there is much more to be gained through studying the similarities. One such similarity between top barrel racers is a *commitment to excellence.* The top 15 barrel racers all follow a different path to rodeos all around the country, but each of them have many of the same "tools" in their trailer. One doesn't just head to Las Vegas with a horse trailer and no map, expecting to compete at the National Finals Rodeo. By the time they get to and stay at top levels, the nation's top barrel racers have developed confidence in the utilization of methods that over time have achieved positive results. Someone who believes they will make it to the Olympics if they just do enough jumping jacks, is kidding themselves. Someone who crosses their fingers in hopes of getting to the top levels of barrel racing without intense commitment and a specific plan, is also.

Not nearly enough barrel racers are specific about *where* they are going and *how* they are getting there. This is especially true when it comes to how our horses move. Trotting the barrel pattern while you add salsa to your mental Wal-Mart list is *not* a representation of intense commitment to excellence. Again, what we get out of our horses in a performance, is only as good as what we put in. In this chapter we'll learn more about "quality movement," why it's so rare (truly a secret) why it's important, and what you can expect when you require it from your barrel horse.

Commitment to Excellence

A formal definition of quality is "Having a high degree of excellence; a state of excelling." As it applies to horses, quality movement is purposeful and intentional versus scattered or dull. To excel in barrel racing, we must specifically ask our horses to move with a high degree of excellence, that is, "quality." When I use the term "quality movement," it's not necessarily an opinion of what I think is quality versus inferior; I think of quality movement as the kind of movement that is more likely to result in excellence as determined in competition.

Strive for excellence in all you do.

This excellence doesn't usually occur by accident – it's something that a winning barrel horse is familiar with delivering all throughout his training, even as he walks the pattern. We can inspire a greater degree of excellence in our horse's movement *if* we know what to look (feel) for.

Like athletic ability in people, when it comes to quality movement, some horses seem to have more natural talent than others. Regardless of how much ability you have to start with, when you understand the key ingredients necessary for quality movement, you can further develop these skills in your horses and reap the benefits on the barrel pattern as a result.

66 No one ever attains very eminent success by simply doing what is required of him; it is the amount and excellence of what is over and above all the required, that determines the greatness of ultimate distinction. 99

— Charles Kendall Adams

Continuity

A first step in developing a horse that navigates the barrel pattern as efficiently as possible comes in setting him up to travel efficiently in general. Rather than trying to coerce a horse into using his body properly, give him a good reason to.

If your horse has ever felt rough or choppy or had tendencies to rush, change speed, direction or gait, then a simple answer may lie in trotting or loping for longer periods. When a horse trots or lopes long enough, they become more skilled and naturally efficient at moving. Once they realize they'll be going for a while, they start to distribute more weight to the hind quarters and maintain speed and direction. As he does so, he benefits by becoming more comfortable and relaxed. As a horse with less talent becomes a more skilled mover, he begins to feel lighter, with less "thud" as his feet contact the ground. When done in this way, moving efficiently becomes the horse's idea, not something we physically impose on him.

- To naturally develop your horse's desire to use his body efficiently, start by asking your horse to trot for five minutes straight while maintaining speed, direction and gait. If your horse speeds up, slows down or veers off track, patiently and persistently guide him back on track until he can maintain better on his own. Based on your horse's fitness level, gradually work your way up to 15 minutes. Do the same at the lope. In doing so you are causing your horse to make a mental shift and decide on his own to use his body differently.

Cadence

Cadence is an often overlooked but critical part of creating quality movement. Defined as "the beat or measure of any rhythmic movement," cadence is the timing of a horse's footfalls. Ideally, the rhythm of our horse's feet is of even tempo. Horses understand and are comforted by various forms of rhythmic motion, which explains why using rhythmic pressure is such an effective way of communicating with them. A rider who is aware of the cadence of her horse's feet can use that to precisely time foot falls and in the process solve issues such as running by barrels or dropping a shoulder. When the transition into a turn is timed properly based on the cadence of a horse's feet, rating becomes easier and stopping and backing up before a turn to teach rate often becomes unnecessary.

When learning to become more aware of your horse's cadence, pay special attention to the inside hind foot. The position of this foot, and the forward even rhythm in which the horse moves can make or break a horse's ability to complete a turn quickly and efficiently.

- To get a feel for cadence, walk around the arena and choose one foot to focus on at a time. Bend over your horse to look at his feet, notice for example when the front left foot hits the ground and then use your bodily awareness to feel it without looking. Experiment with closing your eyes and feeling the moment that left front lands on the ground. Say out loud "Left, left, left." Do the same for all four feet at a walk. Next get a visual of the diagonal movement of the feet at the trot, then feel that movement and count out the beats with your eyes closed. Eventually move up to a lope. Experiment with moving from one point to another repeatedly while counting your horse's steps at the walk, trot and lope each time. Notice whether your horse takes the same amount of steps, and see if you can influence that number while keeping an even tempo.

Impulsion

Some definitions describe impulsion as the powerful thrust that comes from a horse's hindquarters propelling a horse forward, while others define it as pushing power coming from a *desire* to move forward with energy. Yet other sources describe impulsion as the measure of a horse's responsiveness. It's true that a horse uses their hind quarters to generate energy, but that energy isn't generated from a physical place. A horse must first have the *desire* to move energetically. When the desire to "go" and "whoa" is not equal, then your horse will either be impulsive or non-responsive. The best way I can describe impulsion, is that it's not the energy or responsiveness itself, but the measure of it. Simply put, the more response to a cue, the more impulsion we have.

This applies even in cases in which the energy is not directed forward because a horse can also move backward and sideways with impulsion. When a horse responds powerfully and in a timely fashion to cues, it makes any athletic maneuver smoother, more efficient and correct. Minus impulsion, a horse's movements are delayed, flat, heavy, and lacking suspension – any maneuver becomes much more difficult for the horse to perform.

- There are plenty of individuals out there who would suggest some bit and spur therapy for an impulsive or unmotivated horse. There are ways, though to help a horse of either extreme to energetically move forward or gather themselves and stop. We mentioned above that impulsion is considered "the measure of a horse's response to the rider's cues," in any direction so this applies to the degree of "go AND whoa" our horse has. For a horse with a tendency toward "go" spend several sessions focusing on small circles. For the horse with more "whoa" keep the circles to a minimum and try incorporating long, straight lines into your ride. Get out of the arena and head for the hills if you can. Doing so gives each of these types natural motivation to do what you want, which equals less frustration and need for mechanical devices.

- Our horse's responsiveness will only be as light as the pressure we first apply. If we divided the degree of pressure necessary to get a desired response into four phases, one being very light, and four being very firm, it's safe to say that many riders never develop a high degree of responsiveness in their horses because they spend too much time using phases two and three. They don't start light enough and don't get firm enough, when necessary. Less is so much more. Keep in mind that horses are sensitive enough to feel flies land on their skin and that reins are meant more for communication than they are for restraint. If we train a horse to transition upward or downward in gait with extremely subtle cues, if we first train him to softly yield to subtle pressure from a mild bit, then we are taking a huge step forward in ensuring that we never end up with a horse that won't "go" or "whoa" when asked. Always cue a horse by first applying very light (implied) pressure, which may be as subtle as lifting the energy in your body and mentally focusing on what you want. Increase the intensity of the pressure until you receive the desired response and release instantly or go back to the degree of pressure you wish to use to create the desired response. Pressure motivates and the release teaches, but *the firmness* in which we apply pressure and *the timing* in which we release it, makes all the difference.

Shorten & Lengthen

In a barrel racing run there is a lengthening of stride in the straightaways and shortening in the turns, with the transitions needing to happen very quickly. The more skilled your horse is at changing stride length in slow work, the better he will be at doing so in a run.

The distance by which a horse can lengthen his stride varies by individual, but it's ideal for our horse to lengthen as much as possible in between the barrels. When studying the science of speed, you'll be told that a more ground covering stride is faster, even if it looks slower to the eye. This lengthening does not just occur in the limbs, the entire body is involved. So essentially, the horse's entire body, not just the stride, will lengthen. The key here, though, when teaching a horse to lengthen, is that the tempo (cadence) of his foot fall remains the same. A lengthened stride may get a horse from point A to point B faster, but the rate at which his feet move does not quicken. For example, a horse that takes six strides to get from point A to B may take only three with an extended stride. Changing stride length takes strength and balance; it is a skill that must be developed over time. When the ability to change stride length is first developed at slower gaits, it can be done more easily at speed.

- To encourage the lengthening of stride, imagine you are taking steps for your horse. His legs become your legs, as if you're pedaling a bike. Start by lengthening your own "stride" in the saddle and asking your horse to match your rhythm. Be very aware as you ask for this lengthening that the cadence remains the same. Use your hands to gently "collect" any added energy so as to not let it "escape." Once your horse can go back and forth between their normal and extended stride, work on bringing their normal stride length back to shorten it. To do so, take shorter steps as you ride, still imagining that your legs are your horse's legs.

Remember this is all done within the same gait, staying at the same tempo.

- Encourage your horse to lengthen stride by establishing an even cadence, then trot over ground poles placed three feet apart and make it your goal for your horse to take only one step between poles. Move up to a lope with the poles placed six feet apart. After traveling over a series of poles return to a normal stride length before approaching the poles again. Experiment with moving the distance between poles to slightly smaller or larger distances to help your horse learn to shorten and lengthen.

Collection

The time has come to discuss the most talked about, most misunderstood, and most important component in developing the barrel horse – that of collection. All the aforementioned concepts discussed in this chapter and previous chapters are critical to collection – it is not likely to exist in absence of any of them. For a horse to quickly and efficiently navigate the barrel pattern, he must lengthen in the straightaways, shorten in the turns, but maintain a degree of collection throughout.

True collection, is much more than a physical way of moving – it's a total-body feeling and state of mind. When considering the confusion surrounding what collection is, in addition to the fact that most horses and riders are missing the prerequisites for collection, it's not surprising that it seems so difficult and is so rarely achieved.

A horse that is asked to move with collection in slow work is a horse that is more likely to move with collection at speed. A collected horse positions their body to carry more weight on the hind end, lightening up the front end, creating space for hind legs to move further under the body. The horse's neck and head actually raise slightly as the withers elevate. The horse's abdominal muscles engage and the horse lifts and rounds his back. Light contact with the reins captures the body's energy as the horse flexes at the poll and carries himself lightly.

Collection turns a performance horse into a hovercraft, making it possible to change direction, speed or stride length quickly and easily. Collection gives a horse balance and strength in his body to power through a turn or accelerate on the straightaway. Collection is a gathering of energy as the physical body parts also become gathered underneath the horse. Words like big, elevated, strong, energetic and springy all help to describe what collection feels like. When riding a horse that is truly collected, there is a feeling of being actively carried, it's a wonderfully light and effortless feeling, a feeling that unfortunately not many barrel racers are familiar with.

True collection is physical, mental and emotional. The opposite of collection is scattered. A horse that is mentally scattered is not *with* their rider. They may be focused off in the distance or on anything but the task at hand. Their idea and  the rider's idea are not the same idea. A mentally scattered horse lacks leadership and respect; he has not been given good enough reason to mentally focus on his rider and respond to what has been asked. A horse that is emotionally scattered may rush and be chargy or he may show lack of interest and seem lethargic. He may do this out of fear or out of boredom, either way his needs are not being met and his unbalanced emotions leave him unable to fully align with his riders wishes. A horse that is physically scattered is strung out. Improper body positioning allows his energy to escape in various places, such as through a bulging shoulder, dropped rib cage, or hind legs that stretch out behind him.

A horse that is collected mentally is alert and responsive to his rider. His rider has proven herself a worthy leader, and so the horse naturally respects her wishes. An emotionally collected horse is a genuinely-willing horse. He does not try to avoid requests out of fear, and he does not lack enthusiasm due to boredom. He has the right balance of "whoa and go" that equals impulsion. A physically collected horse has the right balance of relaxation and flexion necessary to create a circuit of energy that circulates through both the horse and rider's bodies, creating a gathered, round, balanced way of moving.

Moving in a physically collected way comes easier to some horses, but it comes harder to many horses due to faulty riding or equipment. To encourage a horse to move in a collected way, a rider herself must first be physically, mentally and emotionally collected. The energy must circulate from the rider's feet to the horse's hind quarters, through their back, their mouth, through the reins and riders hands down their body to their feet and back again. The flow of this energy can be blocked by a rider that collapses a certain part of her own body, or by a saddle that pinches or is placed too far forward, limiting freedom of movement and elevation of the front end.

Collection does not require the rider to physically hold a horse in a collected frame. Collection is self carriage, something we teach horses to take responsibility for. If a rider has done her homework up to the point where collection is desired, the horse is familiar with and willing to take responsibility for things such as maintaining direction and maintaining gait, so although it takes time to develop strength for collection, taking responsibility to maintain it should be nothing new.

Bumping or pulling is not necessary from the rider to achieve collection, only steady but giving hands that allow the horse freedom within the light contact. Constant pushing and driving with the legs is also not part of true collection, instead horses carry the responsibility to maintain quality forward movement. If we do our part to regularly require our horses to maintain this quality movement, they are likely to take responsibility for performing with the same quality movement that is signature of a winning run.

So many riders, even those who are certain they know collection when they see or feel it, are sadly mistaken. I for one, realized that what I thought was collection, was not it at all. It was a soft, smooth, but lethargic movement with headset. Collection does not consist of getting a horse to lower their head, flex at the poll and have a soft feel in their mouth. As we are beginning to understand, it's much, much more than that. I had started and trained numerous horses, taken several of them to competition level, without ever having known of true collection. I mention my experience, because I have a feeling that many more are in this state of ignorance, as I was.

> ❝ *You cannot make it as a wandering generality. You must become a meaningful specific.* ❞
>
> – Zig Ziglar

Although there are numerous precursors to true collection, for many barrel racers, when they all come together, it is often the key that will unlock the door to success. Below I've included some steps for starting on your path to teaching collection.

- When teaching collection, keep in mind the many prerequisites. Set yourself up for success by first making sure the horse (and rider) have the foundational qualities in place (described in the previous chapters) that are necessary in order for physical, mental and emotional collection to be a possibility.

- In order to teach collection, one must first have relaxation. Some of us may think of a muscle bound dressage horse as the ultimate form of collection but tension is actually the enemy of collection. Have you ever disciplined your horse and noticed that immediately after, when upset by the reprimand, they (even if temporarily) traveled with their head up, taking short, choppy steps? Their emotions became unbalanced and they developed tension in their body. When a horse demonstrates this state of mental and physical brace – collection is no longer possible.

- Once we have relaxation, we must have lateral and vertical flexion. This flexion is necessary through the body, meaning that a horse must have lateral flexion to bend back and forth. Think of this as the whole-body bend that we ask for as a horse rounds his body around a turn verses a neck that is just "bent." Vertical flexion is necessary to lift their body upward and stretch forward, with a round back, creating space for the hind legs to reach further under the body. Flexion must also be present in the neck and head, first laterally or side to side and then vertically up and down. These understandings when combined with impulsion from the horse and proper body position in both horse and rider will help set a horse up to achieve true collection.

- We can make any maneuver or way of traveling easier for our horses if we can position our bodies in the way we want them to position theirs. To achieve collection rise slightly in the saddle to create space for the horses back to rise up in. Engage your own stomach muscles and slightly round your lower back to inspire your horse to do the same. Bring up your own body's energy as an invitation to the horse to meet that energy. Encourage your horse to elevate and lift the front end by opening and elevating your own shoulders and looking up and forward. Rather than bump or pull, keep a stable but soft and slightly giving feel on the reins. Think of your hands as helping to frame the horse, without holding up or restraining him. Remember, the goal with collection is self carriage, if the horse doesn't take responsibility for this, transition to another gait and invite him again until he can better understand what you're asking and build strength to hold the position longer. If you're struggling, it's most likely that there is a weak area in one or more of the foundational prerequisites. Place your focus there before returning to your efforts at teaching collection.

66 *If everything seems under control,*
you're not going fast enough. 99

— Mario Andretti

Speed Changes Everything

I can't help but for a moment be transported back in time as a popular Cyndi Lauper tune from the early 80's rings in my head. I suppose that in barrel racing, *money* can also change everything; however, this chapter pertains to speed.

As a sport, barrel racing requires a very unique combination of agility, strength, finesse and speed. No other equestrian discipline compares when it comes to the unique joining of these qualities. Other equine sports require high speed, and yet others require athleticism, some require precision, some others also follow patterns, some are timed events, and some are a combination of some of these; because barrel racing consists of all of them, it's quite simply in a class of its own.

The demands placed on barrel horses and riders are unlike those put on any other equestrian athletes. So if our sport requires such a high degree of speed, agility, strength and finesse, it makes sense that if we expect to see results and experience success, we must take everything in this book to the highest level possible. If we think of attaining barrel racing success as baking a cake, adding a dash of solid foundation and a pinch of quality movement for example, simply won't cut it. We must have the full amount of the right ingredients to have a chance at creating something delicious.

A half second may seem insignificant to many people but in barrel racing, it's an eternity. It can mean the different between placing in the 1D and the 2D, a miniscule ½ second can be the difference between a big paycheck and no paycheck for a professional barrel racer. Margins as narrow as a thousandths of a second can be life changing. As barrel racers, it would be in our best interest to learn something more about this thing that puts a unique twist and challenge into everything we know and do with our horses.

The Great Magnifier

The truth about speed, and the challenges it presents, is that it *magnifies everything*. I'll never forget the wakeup call I received after hearing numerous-time reined cow horse world champion Bob Avila mention in a DVD that "putting your horse on a cow will show you how broke they are." Not long after that, I had my first opportunity to try cutting. I was pretty proud of the level to which I had developed my little mare. When I put her on a cow, (a fake cow to start with), she felt horrible! She felt like the most ill-broke horse I'd ever thrown a leg over. Talk about a humbling experience. The reason this occurred was that we had to move back and forth with timing, agility and precision to match the movement of the cow, with more speed than I had ever required. My mare had responded well to everything I had asked of her up to that point. When pushed to a higher level, holes were exposed that I would not have otherwise known existed. Adding speed on the barrel pattern has the same effect.

Seemingly small problems that go otherwise undetected, come out in full force at speed. When these problems show up, it means that something in the foundation is lacking. As speed increases, everything becomes more difficult, whether you're driving a car or riding a horse. The faster you go, the more suppleness, emotional fitness, responsiveness and body control go out the window.

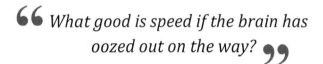

What good is speed if the brain has oozed out on the way?

— Karl Kraus

Speed not only makes it more difficult to perform maneuvers physically, but it raises adrenalin in horses and causes them to become more emotionally fragile as well. If fear and insecurity issues seemed nonexistent before, they can become loud and clear when speed is added, which is good reason to instill solid foundations in our horses and then add speed gradually. If a weakness in our foundation is brought to light, we must be willing to back off the speed and strengthen those areas before going forward. Being aware and understanding of our horse's needs as we add speed can ensure that they are able to confidently handle the added mental, emotional and physical challenges and stress that speed introduces.

The same challenges that occur with speed in horses also occur in riders. Subconscious fears of losing control can come to the surface, causing resistance, hesitation and timing issues. Someone with a seemingly otherwise good seat and soft hands can suddenly morph into "Whiplash the Cowboy Monkey" with the kind of high speed that a winning barrel run requires.

It's been said that if barrel racing was easy, everyone would do it. When we understand the effect speed has, and that it can take everything good we think we have going for us, and turn it into "not nearly good  enough," this simply means that we must do better. We must ask for more responsiveness, instill better foundations and increase emotional fitness in our slower work, if it is to be enough at speed. We must step it up as riders, to be better in every way we can, because speed will always be something that knocks us down lower than where we thought we were.

Barrel racing simply *requires more* of horses *and* riders both. Horses don't lie, and speed doesn't lie. They are the most honest communicators we will come across, but it's up to us to listen. And it's up to us to decide whether we make excuses and point fingers, or if we'll allow the horse and speed to humble us and also inspire us to reach higher levels of excellence. Barrel racing is not a sport for those who prefer to only put forth minimum effort. It's a sport for people willing to go above and beyond, to be challenged, and *still* willing to reach further above and beyond. We'd not only be wise to make sure we had the full amount of all the necessary ingredients for barrel racing success, but we'd be smart to even add extra for insurance. As long as we keep all the ingredients in balance with each other, we'll still have a delicious cake – it will just be extra large in size!

Due to the specific challenges that our speed event presents, it's a good idea to spend time in between barrel runs on spot checking and improving all those foundational qualities that contribute to our success. Many horses, or horse and rider combinations, struggle to overcome the challenges that speed presents. Some horses are more naturally soft and supple at speed, if not, then we may need to spend extra time in that area. A horse that will respond to a light touch in a run, and has great athleticism even at speed, is one that can make instant adjustments in less than ideal circumstances, such as a difficult angle to the first barrel. These horses, who by the way of natural talent or very specific and skillful development, have a major edge in competition.

> 66 *Speed is a great asset; but it's greater when it's combined with quickness — and there's a big difference.* 99
>
> — Ty Cobb

The Science of Speed

The science of speed has been studied in great depth in areas ranging from NASCAR driving to Olympic sprinting. In the world of barrel racing, we haven't come close to touching the surface of the research that has been done in other sporting events. When it comes to the science of speed, for many years barrel racing was in the dark ages.

One of the first to shine a light on this subject was Shane and Lanette Pritchard who brought Tanner Time to the world of barrel racing. Broke into seven sections (three for turns, four for straightaways), Tanner Time comparison reports showed in detail where a barrel racer needed improvement on the pattern. Together with Lynn and Murray McKenzie, the Prichards traveled the US for several years, bringing not only the ability to analyze runs with the help of Tanner Time reports, but also through their labs, they began teaching barrel racers how to make changes that would result in faster times. It was then that the barrel racing community started to pay attention to what Tanner Time was making known. The days of wide pockets had started to fade away and the understanding that straighter, longer is faster took its place and has stood firmly ever since.

Of course, many would argue that each individual has their own style, sometimes featuring a snakey "run around" turn. There will always be exceptions when something that works for a high percentage of the population just doesn't work for certain individuals; in that case it's wise to follow the path that creates the fastest result. The concept of straighter, longer, being faster, although making sense from the get-go, has been proven enough now that it's hard to deny.

The idea behind Tanner Time's findings was that making the "pocket" on the back side of the barrel rather than along side of it, and starting the turn later, would allow the horse to slingshot around a turn while keeping his momentum, much like a ball bouncing off a wall. In effect, their methods didn't necessarily help barrel horses turn faster, but helped them clock faster over all by changing the turn.

Although individual barrel racers may have completed their own experiments in the science of speed, Tanner Time was one of the first and few to bring the knowledge and understanding to the barrel racing public. Until more research is done on the science of speed as it pertains to barrel racing, it's up to us as individuals to do our own research. There is much to be learned from studies done in other sports, even those unrelated to horses. There are two foundational qualities of speed, described below as they pertain to barrel racing:

1. **Movement Efficiency** – How a horse moves, the ability to carry out movement with efficiency.
2. **Horsepower** – The amount of force behind a movement (the difference between a day-old foal and a Thoroughbred race horse sprinting down the track).

Applying the concepts in this book will affect one or both of these two foundational qualities, as will many other methods and techniques. The question to ask then is, "What are the most direct and best ways to improve these two qualities?" When we know the answers to these questions, we can focus our time and effort on those things that are more likely to make the difference we are looking for.

You might ask next, "Just how much of a difference can I expect from my efforts to increase my horse's speed? Is it true that fast horses are born, not made?" Although there is a genetic component involved in running fast, any horse can get faster if trained correctly. To determine which area to focus on, ask yourself - does your horse need more strength (horsepower) or more coordination (movement efficiency)? To define speed, we can break down the science even deeper when we look at the following equation:

Speed = Stride Length x Stride Frequency

Stride Length – the distance covered with each stride
Stride Frequency – the number of strides taken

I can't count the number of times I have laughed and shook my head in amazement as I watched a particularly long strided horse made a wickedly fast run. They look as though they are traveling in slow motion, but one can't argue with how they clock.

The way to improve speed is to either cover more ground, take more steps, or both. Studies have shown that stride frequency is the area that is influenced most by genetics, while stride length is much easier to improve through proper training. So stride length seems to be where it's at when it comes to improving speed. Understanding this is even greater motivation to fine tune our ability to influence our horse's stride length, as described in the *Quality Movement* chapter. In addition, a key to improving stride length comes through proper conditioning – building strength in particular areas of the body that will help a horse overcome his bodyweight, giving them more force or horsepower as he moves through the pattern.

Some additional factors that have been found to contribute most to improving speed are:

Built for speed.

Natural Talent – Some horses are born with natural tendencies to be especially athletic or gifted in certain areas – the area of speed is no exception. Keep in mind though, that when a barrel racer takes it upon herself to study the science of speed and employ strategies for developing a horse to its full potential, it's possible to improve speed in a slower horse to a point that can in some cases even exceed those who are naturally talented. Many horses have never truly been brought to their maximum potential.

Weight – Remember that one of the foundational qualities of speed is horsepower, the amount of force behind a movement. If there is less body mass to move, less force is needed. It's generally said that a "fat horse is a happy horse," which I believe there is some truth to – it's important, however to know where to draw the line between *fat* and *grossly obese*! Weight is a very controllable variable that effects speed. With unnecessary weight being packed around, either in the horse's body or the rider's, it becomes harder to accelerate. In addition, because of leverage, weight, especially that above the horse (in the form of a rider) puts more strain on a horse's body, adding to the difficulty.

Soundness – When a horse is required to use his body for explosive bursts of speed and powerful turns, small soundness issues are going to make a significant difference in how a horse clocks. Although a horse may not be noticeably lame, minor issues like soreness in muscles will cause a horse to be tentative and rearrange his foot placement or use his body differently in response to pain. When this happens, efficiency is lost in small fragments and can results in tenths added to the clock.

Conditioning – Specificity is critical to improving speed in the barrel horse. Although training contributes to a horse's ability to lengthen stride, the biggest gains in stride length come through building strength. It's important to condition the fast twitch muscles for the short bursts of speed that are required in barrel racing. Proper conditioning calls for movements that simulate those that are required in a run as closely as possible. Too many full speed runs, however, can over-stress the horse physically and mentally. Straight line sprints are one way to condition the fast twitch muscles while protecting the horse from excessive wear and tear to the body that frequent turns are more likely to contribute to. In addition, working a horse at ¾ speed is another way to build strength and avoid overdoing it. It's believed to take two months of conditioning for a barrel horse to reach their maximum potential.

Nutrition – A diet that has an imbalance of nutrients will leave the performance horse lacking energy to perform at their maximum potential. The short burst of speed in barrel racing specifically requires that a horse have sufficient stored muscle glycogen. It's important that a horse's diet supports the replenishing of stored glycogen as it becomes depleted through exercise. Adequate fat in the diet is required to provide the slower release of energy necessary in training sessions. Protein is a nutrient necessary to repair muscle. A deficiency of certain vitamins and minerals can cause a variety of health problems and interfere with the proper absorption of nutrients. To rule out deficiencies in a horse's diet, one must first have the forage portion (the bulk of the diet) analyzed to determine where supplementation is necessary. (More information about this process is available in the *Healthy as a Horse* chapter.)

Foot Placement – When it comes to the precise path a horse's feet follow around the barrel pattern, successful horses have varying routes. As previously mentioned, a common theme in the past ten or more years has been the elimination of the "pocket" coming into the turn and the allowance of more room on the backside to create straighter, longer straightaways. The philosophy that the fastest route between two points is a straight line has certainly been proven to ring true in barrel racing. This style has been proven to make the turn easier and more efficient without sacrificing speed. In addition, it allows the horse to stay more upright, balanced, collected in his body and better able to power out of the turns.

Foundation – Every aspect of a horse's foundation and connection with his rider will be put to the test with added speed. Any part of a horse's foundation that is mediocre going slow, will be seriously deficient with speed. In the moments that this becomes clear, time is lost in a run. In order to have success at the highest levels of barrel racing, it's necessary to take all the "secrets to barrel racing success" to the highest level possible for the horse *and* rider. Rather than leave anything to chance, challenge yourself to create insurance for your performance by solidifying all the areas that make up a solid foundation to the best of your ability.

Rider – As we learned in the *Rider Responsibilities* chapter, a rider can seriously get in the way of a horse trying to perform efficiently on the barrel pattern. A rider with subconscious fears of speed or losing control, or even a rider with an extremely laid back personality will transmit an energy that says "hold back" to a horse that may otherwise be capable of high-level performance. A rider that lacks awareness, balance, feel and timing will be more of a hindrance than an asset on the back of a talented barrel horse. Help your horse be his best by focusing on and putting forth effort in becoming the best rider you can be.

66 *First do no harm.* 99

– Hippocratic Oath

Healthy as a Horse

When the National Finals Rodeo barrel racing qualifiers were asked "What was your biggest lesson this year?" they answered:

"Listen to my horse a little better." – Brenda Mays

"Soundness issues put everything in perspective. For instance, I wanted to run Chism in the worst way at Cheyenne but I knew he wasn't ready. I also turned out of Calgary but I learned that it can work out. Stay on track and do what is good for your horses." – Lisa Lockhart

"I learned to listen to my horses a little bit better. I knew something was wrong with Dolly all year and I just couldn't find it. I learned that even if you have to drive a little bit more or put more money into it, you need to go to the vet. clinic that you are most comfortable with." – Jill Moody

At the highest levels of professional barrel racing, these competitors are still learning lessons in regard to horse care. When it comes to horse health, prevention is the best medicine. But how do we know how to help a barrel horse thrive and perform at optimum level? It starts with being a dedicated student of the horse in general and then understanding the unique demands and stresses that barrel horses endure. In addition, it's necessary to become a student of the *individual horses* in our care. The knowledge is available if you are proactive and seek it out. By investing in your own education, you can empower yourself to make confident decisions rather than guessing or being swayed by outer influences that may not always have your horse's best interest in mind.

When interviewed, none of the NFR qualifiers stated that their biggest lesson was that they "took too good of care of their horses." We've learned that to achieve barrel racing success, we must raise our standards of excellence in every area, and horse health is no exception. When it comes to our horse's health, doing enough "and then some" doesn't necessarily mean that we give our horses more of everything they need to be healthy, because in some cases this can do more harm than good. A better policy would be to *learn enough*, and then some. In doing so, we're more likely to avoid expensive vet bills, time consuming treatments, or frustrating layoffs that can sidetrack us on our path to success.

Prevention is more than good medicine, it's one of our most valuable tools for achieving optimum performance on a consistent basis. To develop a champion barrel horse, one must care for him *as if* he is a champion *first*. But this can only be done, *if we know how*.

Maintenance

It's not uncommon for rodeo folks to drive on tires until they are worn bald and eventually blow to bits on the highway. They might get a few more miles out of them than if they were to get a new set when they started showing significant wear; however, along with this policy comes the risk of having a blowout that pulls a rig across the line into oncoming traffic, possibly causing a head-on collision. A blown out tire might tear up the fender of your truck or trailer, costing much more to repair than the cost of replacing the tire. This is risky and dangerous when it comes to tires, but many people take the same approach when it comes to horse care.

Don't see how much mileage you can get out of your horse until he has a "blowout." Take notice of how he's doing as you're going along, much like you'd check the air in your tires on a regular basis. Schedule regular tire rotations and fix slow leaks while they are small and manageable before they create a big problem. Develop the same policy when it comes to horse health and you're likely to receive much more stress-free enjoyment and longevity in the long haul.

Blocks to Optimum Health

When it comes to horse health, don't allow only the latest fads or claims made in advertising to influence your choices. Resist the temptation to lay the responsibility for your horse's health completely in the hands of equine health professionals or feed and supplement companies. Instead, choose sources of information carefully and do your homework. Use your education and intuition to make decisions that resonate with you. Be an advocate for your horse, protect his health and happiness, be his voice. Be willing to go against what everyone else is doing, to do what you feel is right.

In the end, health problems can still occur despite our best efforts. In the aftermath of a major horse-health issue, a solid education makes it more likely that you can look back and say "I did everything possible," rather than "I wish I would have known." In gratitude of everything your horses do for you, take ownership of your ability to gain knowledge and provide them with the very best care possible.

In some instances, no matter how much we know, our horses will present us with mysteries that prove very difficult to solve. It doesn't help matters that horses have evolved to be masters of disguise. Although most domesticated horses today are not faced with the same challenges to ward off predators that their ancestors were, their instincts still go against showing weakness. In addition, when it comes to troubleshooting a health issue, we are faced with the difficulties caused by their sheer body mass. Providing an accurate diagnosis becomes difficult considering the limited degree to which we can see within the horse. In some cases we must opt to treat our horses with therapies based on what we *guess* the problem to be; however, when we are dedicated students, it becomes an *educated guess* – there is a big difference.

Whether we're making decisions on how to best support a winning barrel horse in the making, or if we are troubleshooting an existing health problem, we must do our best to fully understand the pros and cons and risks and benefits that come along with the variety of options available to us.

> 66 *The trick is not in knowing what to do, rather in knowing when to do it. Everything works sometimes, but nothing works every time. If something fails on even ONE horse, then it must be considered a tool, not a rule!* 99
>
> – Cindy Sullivan

Virtually every possible problem that a barrel horse could experience *can* be caused by a health problem (and a whole host of other things of course). When troubleshooting an issue, realize that it's the cause, not just the symptom that needs a resolution. All the intricate systems within a horse are connected, what effects one area, affects another. Keep in mind that just because your horse is not lame, does not mean there is not a health issue. Because your veterinarian examined your horse and confirmed a clean bill of health, does not mean there is still not an underlying health issue.

Outside of lack of education and awareness, a block for many in the way of quality horse care is money, or lack of it. Providing top notch care for a performance horse can be expensive, no doubt. When we take on responsibility for a horse, we also take on risk that the horse will develop health problems or get in an accident that may require massive amounts of time and money to treat. Consider the degree to which your time or financial limits would be stretched in the event of a major health issue. If you ever find yourself skimping on quality health care due to lack of funds, the solution comes in either raising your income or decreasing expenses. It's up to each individual to be honest with themselves and determine if their standards of horse health care can and should be raised, and then decide which option is more feasible and how it will be accomplished.

Another common and unfortunate block in the way of horse health can be the owner's unrelenting drive to win. It's ironic, when it seems obvious that our horse's greatest chance at winning comes when they are feeling their best; however, when a barrel racer makes winning a priority above all else, great sacrifices are often made. A barrel racer might opt to keep competing despite the signs of physical stress, or opt for risky medical procedures in order to keep going down the road rather than allow the horse time off to fully rest and heal. It's not uncommon for horses to experience short or long term pain and discomfort due to the decisions made by their owners. Barrel horses have been pushed to the point of being crippled for life, many have even died in the name of winning.

Whether or not you have ever been in this position, consider how you can avoid putting yourself under that kind of pressure. If you experienced this unhealthy degree of pressure to win, step back and ask yourself - *why*? Peel back the layers and come to terms with the real reason for that pressure. Make sure your personal worth is not attached to being a successful barrel racer. Most of us loved horses before we loved barrel racing. Do your best to make choices that keep their long term health and happiness a priority.

Making sure a horse is truly healthy goes beyond meeting their physical needs, but their mental and emotional ones as well. With these blocks to quality horse health care out of the way, an open mind and desire to learn, we can begin to better understand the basic, core health needs of horses in general, and the specific, unique needs of barrel horses and of your own individual horses.

Learn THE Horse

Although books and other resources have a lot to offer, there is much to be gained by simply studying and watching horses in their environment. We'd be wise to focus both on educational resources to gain knowledge as well as simply listening to the best teacher of all, the one standing in the pasture.

Ask yourself: Do you really know what's going on underneath all that muscle and hair, or do you need to study anatomy and better understand how the parts of their body work together? Are you completely prepared in the event of an emergency that requires you to give a life saving injection? Can you apply a bandage to a leg in a way that will ensure it won't cause damage to the tissues or fall off? Can you spot a balanced shoeing or trim job when you see one? Do you know which diseases your horse is at most risk for when on the road? Do you know the pros and cons of the various deworming protocols available? Do you know what the best ways are to support your horse's immune system? Can you recognize the symptoms of mineral toxicity? Are you confident enough in your own education to choose qualified equine health professionals you can trust? Can you tell the difference between a cough triggered by dust or one caused by a respiratory infection? Do you know when the best time is to check your horse's legs for heat or swelling? Do you know what factors determine whether or not a horse should see a veterinarian for wound treatment? Do you know how to decrease the chances of your horse experiencing colic, ulcers, bleeding, tying up and laminitis?

This book wasn't intended to answer all of these questions for you. In fact, an entire book could be written about each of these areas of horse health. My intent is to ignite a spark, to inspire you to learn the answers to all of the questions above... and much more. If you care about horses, if you want to go to the highest levels of barrel racing, then take matters into your own hands. Empower yourself through strengthening your foundation of knowledge in all aspects of horse health. The extra confidence you'll gain from the inner certainty that you have provided your horse with the best care is only a small part of the return on your investment.

Learn YOUR Horse

Learning your horse starts with spending time with him. *Really learning* your horse begins with high level awareness and spending A LOT of time with him. When a health issue comes up, knowing your horse can be the difference between life and death. At minimum, knowing your horse can save you time, money, worry and spare your horse discomfort.

Ask yourself the following questions: Do you know how much water your horse drinks in a day? Do you know your horse's normal vital signs (respiratory rate, heart rate and pulse)? Do you know what time of day your horse enjoys a nap? Do you know what corner of the pasture he spends most of his time in? Do you know why? What motivates your horse, what is important to him as an individual? Does he usually feel fresh after time off? Does your horse seem especially stressed out in the absence of other horses? Are there certain types of feed your horse doesn't like? Does he get nervous in environments with loud noise? Does your horse perform better on hard or soft, deep ground? Does your horse tend to lose weight when you are on the road? Does your horse run and buck because he feels good or to release stress?

In addition to developing our awareness and spending more time with our horses, remember that when we learn to communicate effectively with them, we can more easily understand what they are telling us, versus just taking a guess. Commit yourself to becoming fluent in their language. Understanding your horse's individual needs will allow you to anticipate them. Knowing what's normal for your horse will help you notice minor problems before they become major, which is all part of keeping them happy, healthy and competitive.

There is a lot we can learn by studying what has contributed to the health of horses over the past few million years; however, the demands we place on our horses today are very different than those placed on horses in earlier stages of evolution. Horses weren't designed to thrive under the stresses that riding, competing and hauling create – which is again, a reason why we must go above and beyond to meet their unique needs. We can also certainly be grateful for modern medicine and the important part it also plays in keeping our horses going strong. It's important to be well versed on the pros and cons involved in our choices. In doing so, we are better able to make decisions that contribute *the most* to keeping our barrel horses in top form while taking on the least amount of risk. To learn more about how to best support the health of our barrel horses, the remainder of this chapter takes a look at those areas where special attention should be paid in order to do just that.

Movement

Why it's Important – Mother Nature intended for horses to move 20 or more miles a day. The common practice of keeping horses in stalls or small enclosures was developed for human convenience. With increased movement comes increased circulation, which is critical for healing and critical to the health of every living thing. When we realize the significant impact adequate movement has on our horse's health, providing them with as much opportunity for movement as possible becomes an easy decision to make.

Symptoms – Without adequate movement our horses can experience delayed healing of injuries, sore muscles, poor hoof health, more risk of respiratory disease, increased occurrence of thrush, less flexibility, as well as

Movement = Circulation = Health

less elastic and resilient muscles, ligaments and tendons, making them more prone to injury. In addition, confinement often causes stress, so lack of movement can also negatively affect our horse's mental well being. Signs of distress can include cribbing, weaving, eating manure, depression and other behavioral issues.

What You Can Do – Does this mean that you should take your blanketed horse in the heated barn and turn him loose with the brumbies? Not necessarily, or "not so fast," anyway. It's true that at the deep core of every horse is an instinctual need for movement and open spaces. It's also true that there are numerous benefits that come from providing your horse with as much space for movement as possible. If a horse was brought up in an environment that did not provide this, however, then he may be conditioned to find comfort in what is familiar to him, which might be a cozy warm stall at night. If you're considering a transition in your horse-keeping practices, be mindful of what your horse has been conditioned to, and remember that horses are stressed by change, and thrive on consistency. When making changes to your horse's living arrangements, it's wise to make any transition process one that takes place over time whenever possible.

66 *When diet is wrong, medicine is of no use. When diet is correct medicine is of no need.* **99**

– Ancient Ayurvedic Proverb

Nutrition

Why it's Important – When horses receive all the nutrients necessary for body processes to operate efficiently, they are better able to meet the various demands of training, conditioning and competing. Providing a balanced diet sets our horses up for success both physically and mentally. In addition, when supported with a balanced diet, the equine athlete is less likely to experience health problems, so although it can enhance performance, it's also a great form of prevention.

Symptoms – Nutritional imbalances, deficiencies and toxicities can be hard to detect. They often exist for extended periods before symptoms develop. Imbalances in the diet can cause inflammation, tying up, nervousness, decreased stress tolerance, a weak immune system, poor wound healing, increased infections, bone and joint abnormalities, arthritis, muscle cramps, weakness, dehydration, dry skin, poor hair coat, poor hoof quality and loss of appetite. In addition, imbalances in one area can actually prevent the proper absorption of other nutrients, leading to more imbalances. Don't be fooled into thinking a horse is healthy from the inside out based on his appearance alone. A processed feed that causes a horse to have a shiny coat, can also include ingredients that are detrimental to his health.

What You Can Do – The nutritional analysis on feed bags is not particularly valuable information unless one knows how the main portion of the diet (forage – hay or pasture) is lacking. Finding out the nutrient content of your hay or pasture is relatively easy and is made possible by providing a hay or grass sample to a company such as EquiAnalytical (www.EquiAnalytical.com) for testing. Consider consulting with an equine nutritionist to balance a diet for you based on the requirements set by the National Research Council and the forage test results you provide. No "perfectly balanced" processed feed from the store is likely to meet your horse's need for specific amounts of more than 30 nutrients, minerals and vitamins, which are already being provided in varying levels through the bulk of his diet.

The horse's digestive systems are not adapted to digesting large quantities of carbohydrates. Digestion of starch (grain) products creates lactic acid build-up, and too much can drop the pH level in the digestive system and can cause fermentive overload in the hind gut. This can lead to loss in body condition, tying up and digestive upsets such as colic. Too much starch in the diet is also believed to cause weakness in the structures of the hoof. The less grain we have to feed, the less likely our horse is to experience the health issues mentioned above. For this reason, it becomes even more important to find and purchase the best quality hay possible in order to decrease the dependence on grain to balance the diet.

Balancing a diet may require mixing your own feed and customizing a mix of supplemental minerals. It's not as much work as it sounds and the benefit of having a feeding program you can be confident is meeting your horse's nutritional needs is certainly worth the effort. When your horse eats only quality feed without all the lesser quality ingredients and by-products he doesn't need, his body will operate more efficiently and he'll actually need to eat less, quite possibly lowering your feed bill.

Conditioning

Why it's Important – A well conditioned barrel horse will have a competitive edge for several reasons. Conditioning improves circulation which improves the body's ability to rid muscle tissue of metabolic waste (lactic acid, CO_2), reducing soreness. With fewer waste products in the blood, respiration becomes easier, allowing for greater oxygen intake, necessary to supply energy. As the body's systems work more efficiently, the horse is better able to rid his body of excessive heat as well. Better fitness also means improved neuromuscular coordination, meaning they are better able to perform the specific skills required for barrel racing. They will essentially have greater strength with which to move their body mass, resulting in increased speed. In addition, a horse that has developed strong muscles, tendons and ligaments is less likely to experience tears, sprains, strains and other injuries.

Symptoms – A horse that is out of shape will sweat more than a fit horse and struggle with maintaining a healthy body temperature, making him more at risk of overheating. Because his bodily systems are not operating at maximum efficiency, he will also experience an elevated respiratory and heart rate as the body struggles to deliver nutrients and oxygen required for energy. His body will fatigue more quickly which can cause him to overextend himself or take a misstep. An out of shape horse is not able to rid his body of waste efficiently, and although not always perceptible to the eye, soreness can result in addition to tying up.

What You Can Do – There are many different schools of thought when it comes to conditioning the barrel horse. Some barrel racers develop and follow structured exercise programs for their horses that include a gradually increasing duration of walking, trotting and loping, so many days a week. For many, conditioning schedules are determined by the specific needs of each individual horse. Whatever kind of conditioning program resonates with you, there are a few basic concepts to keep in mind.

- Warm Up – An adequate warm up period before exercise helps insure your horse's muscles, tendons and ligaments stay healthy by increasing elasticity and flexibility, (think Laffy Taffy) lessening the likelihood of injury.
- Cool Down – Walking a horse to cool them out after a workout promotes circulation which is necessary to rid the body of waste products produced during exercise that may otherwise lead to soreness.
- Fatigue – A tired horse is more likely to take a misstep, stumble, overexert or overextend himself. Lessen a horse's chance of injury by not pushing him further than his current fitness level allows. Allow for adequate recovery time during exercise sessions and in the days between more challenging workouts.
- Condition for your Event – To receive the most benefit from a conditioning program, incorporate some fast practice runs and/or sprints (as you horse's fitness level allows) to simulate the movements required by your horse in competition. Doing so not only helps your horse build strength specific to barrel racing, but can also reduce the risk of injury. At the same time, be mindful that you don't over condition and create more physical and mental stress than your horse can sufficiently handle.

Hoof Care

Why it's Important – The old saying still rings true "no hoof, no horse." The feet are the foundation of the entire horse; when they are not healthy the health of the whole horse is compromised. When this is the case, lameness can result. Lameness causes pain and stress, limits movement, contributing even more to the loss of health for the entire horse; however, lameness does not have to be present for poor hoof health to exist. Hoof problems are silent killers. This is often because many horse owners are unable to differentiate between a healthy foot and an unhealthy one, therefore problems are not recognized until late stages.

Symptoms – An unhealthy foot is one that may have visual signs such as cracks, chips, flares, thrush, white line disease or abscesses. The hooves may be dry, shelly, brittle or may be overgrown with separated hoof wall and underrun heels, or be overgrown at an extremely upright angle with false soles. Inflammation may be present, or thin soles may make the horse prone to bruising and cause a horse to travel tentatively on hard surfaces. Many hoof issues go unnoticed because it's the inner structures that are weak or compromised. Examples include a coffin bone that has shifted to varying degrees within the hoof capsule, changes to the navicular bone and under developed digital cushions and lateral cartilages. Unbalanced trims or shoeing can result in muscle soreness, inflammation and stress to various parts of the body.

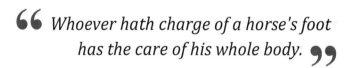

❝ *Whoever hath charge of a horse's foot has the care of his whole body.* **❞**

– Unknown

What You Can Do – A horse's foot was designed to work like a blood pump, supplying necessary oxygen and nutrients to the extremities as it expands and contracts slightly with each step the horse takes. The more movement a horse is allowed, the more blood flow increases and strengthens the inner structures of the hoof, contributing to the development of a healthy, thick, callused sole. In addition, the expansion and contraction of a bare hoof as it contacts the ground allows it to work as a natural shock absorber, lessening wear and tear to joints, adding to a horse's longevity. These are all reasons why many farriers agree that a horse's feet

Taking matters into my own hands.

are healthiest without rigid shoes - they interfere with the way the feet were meant to function.

A diet high in sugar and starches (grain, sweet feeds) will weaken hoof structures, making laminitis and white line disease more likely. Many horses have thrush (even those in dry environments) without their owners realizing it. As long as thrush exists, the degeneration of the protective hoof callous it causes will always prevent the hoof from being the picture of optimum health.

Common horse keeping habits such as the application of shoes, restriction of movement and the feeding of high starch diets are all ways in which we actually stand in the way of hoof health, and the health of the horse as a whole. I encourage all barrel racers to educate themselves and study the anatomy and function of the hoof and make their own educated decisions when it comes to providing hoof care.

Joint Support

Why it's Important – Supporting healthy joint function is critical due to the excessive physical demands placed on barrel horses.

When a joint becomes inflamed and the inflammation continues for a period of time, the smooth cartilage covering the bone starts to break down. The body reacts by laying down extra bone in the joint as an effort to prevent additional stress in that area. Once established the process causes discomfort and eventually leads to lameness and arthritis. If we want our horses to have full, pain free utilization of the joints, it's necessary to prevent this disease process from occurring.

Symptoms – Irritation, inflammation and cartilage damage in the joint often go unnoticed because the horse doesn't show symptoms right away. In early stages, swelling and heat may be noticed, as well as stiffness after exercising or after standing for long periods. When lameness finally does show up, it's been something in the making for quite a period of time, even if it seems to appear suddenly. A horse that was once working well and then starts hesitating to enter the arena, blows out of a turn or has a choppy or bouncy stride around the barrel, could possibly be experiencing joint pain. Joint pain can also be responsible for decreased speed and agility, problems with stride, lead changes, resistance and behavior problems, tension in the body when ridden, high head carriage and even digestive problems.

What You Can Do – Other than an acute injury, there are many causes for inflammation in the joint. They may include repeated trauma and stress caused by unbalanced shoeing, ill fitting saddles, unbalanced or excessive weight bearing and poor confirmation. Because a barrel horse's joints are under excessive stress, and because inflammation can be difficult to detect, it makes sense to take steps to support healthy joint function as a preventative measure.

It seems as though joint injections are becoming so common place in the performance horse world that some veterinarians are using them as a diagnostic tool. Rather than digging deep to determine the cause of lameness, some professionals recommend joint injections to see if the horse shows improvement. Many barrel racers schedule their horses for regular joint injections and even consider it as a form of maintenance.

Joint injections do not come without risk. With each entrance by a needle into the joint capsule there is a possibility that bacteria will be introduced. The degree of inflammation caused by an infection can cause permanent damage to a joint. Outside of the risk of infection is the questionable belief held by numerous equine health professionals that the repeated injection of a steroid (meant to decrease inflammation) can actually cause more damage to the joint than it prevents. If joint injections are thought to be necessary, review the options and reasons for doing so carefully.

There are options outside of injections that work toward decreasing inflammation, making it less likely for the body to react to joint stress by laying down extra bone, and damaging the joint. In addition, they promote joint health through supporting the production of healthy hyaluronic acid, which is the lubricating fluid within a joint, necessary for free and comfortable movement.

Oral supplements containing either natural or synthetic ingredients or a combination of them are one such option. Although many horse owners swear by certain oral supplements, there are relatively few studies that have proven their effectiveness. There are also products that can be given via intramuscular (IM) and intravenous (IV) injection. In addition, one such product (Adequan) claims to not only support healthy joint cartilage but also heal cartilage that is already damaged. Some of these options are available via veterinarians while some are over the counter.

Whether you opt to go with an oral supplement, an intramuscular, intravenous or intra-articular injection, first understand specifically how a product works, the benefits and potential risks and side effects that come with each. In addition, keep in mind that some of the most effective and least risky forms of joint support are providing adequate movement, quality hoof care, well fitting tack, proper conditioning, a balanced diet and adequate time off for rest and rejuvenation.

Soft Tissue Support

Why it's Important – Soft tissue injuries are one of the most common causes of lameness in performance horses. They include injuries to the muscles, tendons (strains), which are the fibrous cords attaching muscle to bone, and ligaments (sprains), which is a fibrous tissue that attaches bone to bone or cartilage. Soft tissue injuries can be difficult to diagnose and can take considerable time to heal.

Symptoms – Heat, swelling and lameness are actually the most common and noticeable symptoms of damage to soft tissues. These symptoms can have a sudden onset in the case of an acute injury or can occur over the course of time as lower grade disruptions to the fibers develop. Outside of lameness, heat and swelling, horses with soft tissue damage or injury may show muscle sensitivity and soreness, muscle imbalance and atrophy, stiffness and resistance.

Problems with the feet, or the joints, lack of proper conditioning, etc. can cause damage to the soft tissue over time. When horses experience soft tissue damage, they develop compensatory ways of moving to protect themselves, so a problem in one area is likely to eventually cause a problem in other areas. Discomfort caused by a soft tissue injury can be responsible for decreased speed and agility, problems with stride, lead changes, resistance and behavior problems, tension in the body, high head carriage when ridden, as well as digestive problems.

What You Can Do – Injury to the soft tissues can be caused by external trauma such as a kick from another horse or mechanical overload when the fibers in the tissues are stretched beyond their capacity and rupture. Mechanical overload is more likely to occur

in an unfit or fatigued horse, one being ridden on unsafe ground, one with unbalanced feet, or in the event of a stumble or slip. Many horse owners mistakenly assume that if their horse is lame or sore that they must be experiencing joint pain, when actually soft tissue injuries are more often the cause. When a horse suffers from a soft tissue injury, we want to interrupt the natural disease process, promote healing and return full use to the affected area.

As with the disease process in joints, a horse's body also naturally responds to soft tissue injuries in ways that aren't in line with being sound and fresh for the next barrel race. When the soft tissues are damaged, the body essentially says, "Ouch, we overdid it, let's make sure we don't overdo it again." As swelling quickly sets in, scar tissue is formed as the body tries to heal itself with the intention of restricting use of that part of the body to prevent further injury in the future. The more inflammation there is, the more scar tissue will develop.

Powerful Healing for Soft Tissue Injuries

Of course we want to support healing, but the difference is that we want to bring back *full use* and pain free range of motion to the injured area. Most of the body therapies available to horses, such as massage, acupuncture, chiropractic, hot/cold therapy and magnets, all work toward accomplishing that, and more. Not only can these therapies support a horse with an injury but they can help condition soft tissues to make injury less likely and increase freedom of movement and flexibility, as well as circulation which helps deliver healthy cells to the body parts and remove waste products.

Time & Movement – The one healing modality that perhaps stands ahead of all others is simply time. There are many contraptions and body therapies available to support performance horses, but once the initial injury response is under control, there is nothing that quite compares to the healing power of simple turnout. With the exception of a few types of injuries and horses, time combined with movement can be a powerful combination for healing not only the body but the mind, as movement and wide open spaces cater to a horse's physical and mental needs. Horses can receive rejuvenation from head to hoof through the experience of a good, long pasture vacation.

Mental Health – When it comes to overcoming injury, there is no downplaying the power our mental and emotional state has to either promote or delay healing. Imagine that you've experienced a major injury to your leg, requiring that you stay in bed for weeks. Visualize how the healing process would take place if the room was dark, and if you had no books, no flowers, no TV and no visitors. Now imagine how your body's healing power would be amplified with access to sunlight, fascinating books, funny movies and stimulating conversations with friends.

Depression brought on by confinement might be inevitable in the case of some equine injuries. In these situations, there is usually a lot we can still do to meet our horse's needs to the best of our abilities. Doing so will positively impact their mental and emotional health, opening them up to receive a healing power much greater than what can be provided through treatments and drugs alone.

The body therapies, tools and techniques mentioned below play an important role in healing, but are also very valuable for *maintaining* a healthy, sound barrel horse.

Chiropractic – Chiropractic adjustments work toward removing interference in the transmission or communication from the brain to the various parts of the body via the central nervous system through restoring bones that are subluxated or misaligned to their normal position.

Massage – Equine massage is a therapy used with the goal of enabling the body to use itself with the upmost efficiency. It involves improving circulation and releasing restrictions in the body's soft tissues commonly caused by stress or injury in the performance horse.

Acupuncture – Inside our bodies is an intricate web of electrical circuits called meridians. Acupuncture or acupressure therapy works through mediating endorphins, the body's regulating chemicals. As this is accomplished the body is better able to operate at maximum efficiency.

Stretching – A staple in the warm up routine of human athletes, stretching prepares the body for exertion by making the muscles, tendons and ligaments more flexible and elastic, reducing the risk of injury. To avoid over stretching, utilize "treat stretches," which prevent the horse from going beyond his own comfort zone.

Magnets – Magnets are thought to increase circulation, which is vital to healing and the health of all animals. Adequate circulation can benefit the performance horse by efficiently removing toxins and waste products that are produced in the body through exercise.

Ice – Cold therapy causes blood vessels to constrict, which moderates the body's way of overreacting to stress or injury at a cellular level. Constriction of the blood vessels helps interrupt the natural injury repair process through moderating the release of waste cells to the stressed or injured areas, reducing pain and swelling.

Heat – Heat dilates blood vessels resulting in improved circulation, relaxing soft tissues and improving elasticity. The application of heat encourages the flow of healthy cells important to heal stressed or injured areas.

Infrared and/or Photonic Light Therapy – New in this area are blankets, wraps and other products featuring heat reflective ceramic particles fused into the fibers. In addition to photonic lights, these products, deliver not just any heat, but long-wave infrared heat radiation, which is well documented to reduce pain, increase circulation and promote healing.

Dentistry

Why It's Important – Equine dentistry is not only important for preventing sharp points on the teeth from creating sores inside the mouth. This is yet another area, in which the balance and health of the mouth can support the health of the entire animal. A balanced mouth is one in which the jaws are able to move without restriction as the horse moves and flexes laterally and vertically. When this freedom from restriction is accomplished, it allows for greater freedom of movement in the entire body. Providing appropriate dental care is a necessary part in improving overall health, well-being and maintaining longevity and is key to bringing out a horse's full potential.

Symptoms – A horse with a dental issue can show a wide variety of symptoms that many would be surprised to learn are actually connected to a dental problem. Some more obvious signs are weight loss, slow eating, dropping of food, tilting of the head while eating or when riding, resistance to the bit, gapping of the mouth, head tossing and tail wringing. Some other symptoms of dental problems can even include bucking, running off and a wide variety of other behavioral problems.

What you Can Do – Although often over looked, annual dental exams are a part of good horse care. Performance horses may require a dental check up every six months. In the absence of outward symptoms, a good equine dentist can recognize issues in the mouth that may be contributing to problems in other areas of the body.

When choosing your equine dentist, do so with care. Heat from power tools can permanently damage teeth, making them susceptible to infection. Overly aggressive techniques can affect the viability (life) of the tooth and essentially do more harm than good. There are different schools of thought when it comes to equine dentistry, do your homework and determine which type of techniques resonate with you before scheduling an appointment with a professional.

Ulcers

Why it's Important – New studies have revealed that as many as 90% of performance horses suffer from ulcers. Compared to a human, a horse's stomach is very small for his size. A horse's stomach consists of two parts. The lower part, or glandular region, is lined with a protective tissue that makes ulcers less common in this area. The upper part, the non-glandular region, does not have this protective coating. Humans secrete stomach acid when they eat, horses on the other hand secrete this acid necessary for digestion at all times. When they eat, the saliva that is produced works to buffer the acid. When a horse goes for extended periods without food, the excess acid is believed to damage the stomach lining – causing painful ulcers.

Symptoms – Some symptoms of ulcers are mild colic, poor appetite, weight loss, teeth grinding, diarrhea, poor body condition, behavioral changes, lying down more than normal, poor hair coat, poor performance and behavioral problems. It's believed that stress is a cause of ulcers, but because it's hard to measure, there is not much data existing on this. Studies have found horses whose stomachs were in excellent condition while in what might be perceived as very stressful situations and horses who were turned out on pasture, with severe ulcers.

What You Can Do – Some believe that the hydrocholoric acid in the horse's stomach moves around more so during exercise and trailering, causing horses that are ridden and hauled on a consistent basis to be at higher risk. It's also believed that pain caused by ulcers can flare up under stressful conditions, which could contribute to any anxiety, nervousness and behavior issues that occur before, during or after competition. If you suspect ulcers, it's a good idea to have your horse scoped by an equine veterinarian for a definite diagnosis. Because many veterinary clinics do not have the equipment necessary for this costly procedure, it would be wise to do everything possible to prevent ulcers from ever becoming an issue.

The saliva produced when a horse chews helps to buffer the potentially damaging stomach acid. Eating roughages requires more chewing, therefore produces more saliva. So rather than provide a couple feedings a day, get creative and think of ways to set up slow feeding systems or find turn out options for your horse, to keep food in their stomach as often as possible. Give non-steroidal anti-inflammatory drugs sparingly, (such as bute) as they contain an ingredient that has been shown to increase the amount of acid produced. Do your best to meet your horse's needs and provide a lifestyle for your horse that is as stress free as possible. Doing so will support the natural health of the digestive system, which is absolutely critical to the health of a horse as a whole.

Infectious Diseases

Why it's Important – Infectious diseases are those in which one horse can get from another horse, or a vector, such as a mosquito. Vaccines are a biological preparation of either a weakened or killed strain of a particular virus, bacteria or it's toxins that will stimulate an immune response when administered to a horse. This causes the horse to build antibodies against a particular disease, providing protection, although no vaccine is 100% effective. Most vaccines will provide an adequate immune response 10 – 14 days following the vaccination, depending upon whether the horse has been vaccinated before. Frequency of vaccination depends on each individual horse and how much exposure they receive to certain diseases.

Symptoms – Horses with an infectious disease can show symptoms such as fever, nasal discharge, cough, increased respiration rate, labored breathing, sweating, weakness and general lethargy. Additional symptoms can be stiffness, muscle spasms, ataxia (un-coordination, stumbling, or limb weakness), excitability or disorientation as well as increased salivation, loss of appetite, rapid weight loss, diarrhea and difficulty with urination or defecation. In addition, infectious disease can cause swelling of the lymph nodes under the jaw, abortion in mares and anemia.

What You Can Do – The American Association of Equine Practitioners (AAEP) recommends five core vaccinations annually. They protect against three mosquito born diseases – Eastern Equine Encephalomyelitis, Western Equine Encephalomyelitis, and West Nile Virus. The remaining two core vaccinations recommended by the AAEP are Tetanus and Rabies. In addition they recommend several other vaccines based on risk to protect against Equine Herpes Virus (Rhinopneumonitis), Equine Influenza, Potomac Horse Fever and Strangles.

In recent years, concern has been growing among holistic equine veterinarians and horse owners alike over the possible links that have been identified between what is thought to be over-vaccination and health issues such as hoof abscesses, laminitis, hypothyroidism, hormonal imbalances, allergies and more.

If you question whether vaccination for certain diseases is necessary consider asking your vet to draw a blood sample to submit an antibody titer, which is a test that measures the amount of antibodies in the bloodstream at a given time for a certain disease. It's questionable whether these titers deliver an accurate representation of the protection level, however because they measure only humoral (liquid) immunity (the kind of immunity that spikes after exposure to a disease) and not cellular immunity (long lasting immunity). Before you consider dropping your vaccination schedule all together, be mindful that countless unvaccinated animals have died over the years of preventable diseases. Take a close look at all areas of horse health and do your best to support a healthy immune system through close attention to nutrition and management practices. Discuss your vaccination schedule with a trusted veterinarian and make the well-being of your horse a top priority as you consider your options and arrive at a conclusion.

Parasites

Why it's Important – Sometimes what we can't see, can hurt us in a big way. This is especially true for our horses when it comes to internal parasites. Parasites (or worms as they are so affectionately known) are small organisms that live a portion of their life cycle in the organs, body cavities and tissues of host animals. These free loaders can place a horse's life in danger when found in large numbers and at minimum steal nutrients by feeding on the host animal. Horses can be affected in numerous ways and varying extents by many different species of parasites.

Symptoms – Many horses have dangerous parasite loads without showing outward symptoms. For this reason, it's a good idea to have a fecal egg count completed by your veterinarian (or go to www.HorsemensLab.com). Keep in mind that sometimes, parasites exist in the body but the eggs do not show up in the manure. Some symptoms of an unhealthy parasite load are a dull coat, lack of energy, weight loss, loss of condition, loss of appetite, coughing and/or nasal discharge, tail rubbing, hair loss, depression, diarrhea and colic.

What You Can Do – The first defense comes in management of your horse's living conditions. Avoid overpopulating pastures which requires horses to eat shorter forage closer to the ground, causing the ingestion of more parasite eggs or larva in the process. Remove manure from the horse's environment as often as possible to reduce exposure to parasite eggs. For manure to be completely safe to spread on pasture without risk of spreading parasites, it must be properly composted. Proper composting requires turning piles and in some climates, watering. If this is not an option, try to spread and harrow manure in pastures during dry, hot weather, when the elements are most likely to kill parasites and wait two weeks before turning horses out. Mixed grazing (cattle and horses) can help to disrupt the equine parasite life cycle.

There are pros and cons to chemical dewormers and the frequency at which they are administered. Research has shown that horses can develop resistance to them and some equine health professional believe that the toxic ingredients found in chemical dewormers (necessary to kill the parasites) can have a negative impact on horse health. Due to this, more and more horse owners are utilizing fecal egg counts and employing more natural methods of parasite control such as feeding diatomaceous earth. It's believed that chemical dewormers can cause digestive disturbances, so if going this route try to avoid administering dewormer at times of high stress. Again in this instance, education is a key factor in determining which method of parasite control is right for you and your horses.

Colic

Why it's Important – Colic is the number one killer of horses. Colic is simply defined as abdominal pain, which is actually a symptom rather than a diagnosis. The actual cause of the pain can be wide and varied, but understanding and preventing colic is critical because it can be fatal. Many cases of colic are caused by a gastrointestinal disturbance such as a buildup of gas, a twist of the colon or a blockage just to name a few. Some cases of colic require abdominal surgery to correct, which is no easy feat for a horse, it's expensive and requires major after care.

Symptoms – It's possible for situations that end up in colic to actually begin with uncontrollable muscle spasms due to the effects overexertion and stress have on the equine digestive systems. Ovarian pain in mares is another common occurrence that can resemble colic. Common symptoms are pawing, stretching, frequent attempts to urinate, flank watching, nipping at the stomach, pacing, repeated lying down and rising, rolling, groaning, excess salivation, loss of appetite, decreased fecal output, increased pulse or respiratory rate and dark mucus membranes (gums). If your horse exhibits any symptoms of colic, it's critical that you monitor him closely. Getting medical treatment in a timely manner can be the difference between life and death.

What You Can Do – Again in this area, prevention is the name of the game and there are numerous things we can do as horse owners to make colic less likely. Because horses are naturally designed to digest forages, feed the least amount of grain possible (refer to the section on Nutrition). Provide adequate drinking water to help prevent dehydration. Develop a program for parasite control and provide proper dental care. Make any transitions in feed gradually so as not to upset their sensitive digestive system. Think twice before feeding already compacted feeds in the form of pellets or cubes and provide as much turn out, natural foraging and movement as possible. Be aware of heat cycles in mares and avoid overexertion.

Saddle Fit

Why it's Important – As years go by, and competition gets tougher, we start looking more closely at the little things that can make a difference in competition. For many years, saddle fit was thought of as a "little thing" but if your horse could speak, he would likely object – *it's a BIG thing!* An ill fitting saddle can not only cause soreness, but cause compensatory soreness in other areas of the body. A saddle that pinches at the withers area will restrict free movement of the shoulders, decreasing a horse's ability to accelerate. A saddle that does not properly distribute pressure will discourage a horse from bending and traveling in a collected manner. Many barrel racers place their saddles too far forward, which transfers excessive weight on the forehand, making it more difficult to properly utilize the hind quarters.

A horse that experiences discomfort every time he is ridden is a horse that will grow to resent being ridden. A well performing horse is a comfortable horse. A poor fitting saddle can cause soundness issues and can basically hold a horse back from reaching his greatest athletic potential.

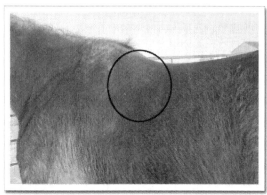

Poor saddle fit has caused this horse to develop muscle atrophy behind the shoulders.

Symptoms – A horse showing symptoms of poor saddle fit may be sore in the back, show muscle atrophy behind the shoulders, be hypersensitive to brushing and have white hairs around the withers. They may show behavior problems such as bucking, a tendency to rush or feel chargey, unwillingness to move forward and pin the ears or bite when saddled. Horses experiencing discomfort due to poor saddle fit might toss their head when ridden, swish their tail, grind their teeth or travel with restricted movement in the shoulders, have shortened stride, a hollow back and high head carriage.

What You Can Do – There are some contradicting opinions out there when it comes to the science of saddle fit. There is much more to it than throwing your saddle on your horse without a pad. After all, you ride *with* a pad, and you ride the horse *in motion*. A saddle that appears to fit on a bare back, while standing still is not likely to fit a back with a pad, and a rider, in motion. The problem with many saddles is that they are too narrow in the gullet or have inappropriate bar angles, causing pinching, pain and restricted movement.

When a saddle fits properly, the weight of the rider will be distributed evenly and the saddle will provide minimal restriction to the horse's movement. Also keep in mind that a horse's back and shape to their top line can change from year to year and season to season or as they build muscle or gain and lose weight. Check saddle fit by slipping your hand under the pad both before it's cinched up and after to feel for pressure points. Step back and look from the side to determine if the saddle sits level on the horse's back. Do this regularly to ensure that what fit once, still fits or whether you need to use shims or pads to correct minor issues or if a different saddle is necessary.

*When it comes to horse health, it seems there is never a shortage of advice available. Make sure the information you receive comes from a trusted source. One such resource is the American Association of Equine Practitioners (AAEP) web site, which includes many valuable articles for horse owners based on traditional veterinary medicine. Visit their web site at www.AAEP.org.

66 *The power of one is above all things the power to believe in yourself. Often well beyond any latent ability previously demonstrated. The mind is the athlete, the body is simply the means to use it.* 99

– Bryce Courtenay

The Inner Game

Just as in tennis, or any other sport, there is an inner and outer game to barrel racing. The outer game is the race against competition, or the clock. Our inner game is played within our minds. If we don't learn ways of mastering our inner game, it can block the achievement of peak performance. In the most basic sense, these blocks take the form of self-doubt and anxiety. When we're able to turn around self-doubt and transform pre-race anxiety, it will benefit us in all aspect of our lives, not just in competition. To understand *why* the inner game of barrel racing is so critical, it helps to first understand how the magnificent piece of machinery between our ears works.

The brain has two hemispheres – we might refer to them as the left brain and right brain, the teller and the doer, the conscious and the subconscious, or the thinking side and the reacting side. Research shows that people tend to either be left brain or right brain dominant. Most of us spend the majority of time in a left brain state, in which we are rational, calculating, verbal, etc. When using our right hemisphere we are more intuitive, spatially aware and creative. This explains why some people can paint beautifully but have trouble with simple addition, or that some people easily understand calculus, but struggle with a one page essay.

In competition, the right brain mode is the ideal place for an athlete to be mentally. This is especially true in the fast paced event of barrel racing, where there simply isn't time to think, analyze and calculate out each move. We need well developed right brain abilities to be aware, feel and react appropriately in the moment, without excessive thought.

This is also where muscle memory comes into play; it's when we subconsciously revert to familiar habits, without having to think about it. Every time we do something new, we create a new neural pathway in the brain, which is a mode of communication between the brain and body. As we repeat certain movements or thoughts, the pathways become more well traveled, making it more likely that we'll keep up with habits, good or bad, once they are established. This explains why it can be difficult to change a certain aspect of our riding, especially in a run where speed is involved. Often times, our left brain thoughts are just too darn slow. The neurons fire in our brain on the same 'ol pathways, causing our body to repeat that habit. It's certainly possible to employ the left, thinking side of the brain to help change these habits and form new "muscle memory," for a better foundation of riding skills; however, the ultimate way to win the inner game of barrel racing lies in developing our right brain capabilities to such a level, that we aren't quite as dependent on muscle memory. After all, let's face it, each run is not exactly the same. Each circumstance, each horse, each run, requires that we are *in the moment* and make subtle adjustments accordingly – in those tiny *fractions of a second*, when it really matters.

With this understanding comes good news and bad news. The bad news is that most of us have an overly active left hemisphere and underdeveloped right hemisphere. The good news is that much like how we condition our horses physically, we can also condition ourselves mentally to better utilize the right side of our brain. This is done through developing our abilities to quiet our "teller" and trust our "doer."

Of course, as with anything else, there are obstacles that can get in the way of utilizing our minds to benefit us in competition. In this chapter we'll look closely at what the most common blocks are and what can be done to overcome them. Included are specific techniques for quieting the overly active left brain mental chatter as well as developing and trusting the right brain abilities to take over and respond appropriately.

The blocks that can get in the way of mastering our inner game are wide and varied in nature, but they tend to fall under the categories of either self-doubt or anxiety. You might think of self-doubt and anxiety as an infestation of bugs in the software of our mind. To get rid of the bugs permanently, we must first know more about them – where they come from, how they got there, what they feed on, and what tactics we can use to overcome them. We have the power to transform these glitches into self-belief and confidence. But unless we know the source of our self-doubt and anxiety, and how to eradicate these "bugs," we'll be continuously plagued by this infestation in our minds.

Fear – the Root of all Evil

When we peel back the layers of self-doubt and anxiety, or any form of interference in our inner game, what we find, albeit often subconscious in form, is fear. We should know that not all fear is bad. Sometimes fear is very valid, it's what keeps us safe. It's not uncommon to develop subconscious self-preservation tendencies that may have been necessary to keep us safe in the past, but no longer serve us. We may fear losing control, or fear what other people think, fear making a mistake or even fear success, without ever really experiencing a conscious thought saying "I'm afraid," as we saddle up or head down the alley. These fears can drastically interfere with our ability to ride and have "feel." They keep us in our left brain mode, making it difficult to be in the moment, and generally stand as a big block in the way of our barrel racing success. This makes sense of why so many barrel racers struggle, even when they seem to be doing so many things right, they're completely oblivious to these sneaky fears.

This fear is something that didn't exist when we were babies, in our purest form. For example, as we were learning to walk, we didn't hold back for fear that we would fall or fear that our peers would think  we were a klutz. We didn't fear that we would *never* learn to walk or that we would never amount to anything if we didn't. We just kept on trying because we didn't yet know fear. As we grew up, life happened. As it did, we were cautioned to be realistic, fear took hold and applied limits, we hesitated, and it capped our greatest potential and robbed us of our innocent belief that we really can do anything. Don't get depressed just yet, because I have more good news – the fear that causes us to doubt ourselves, that holds us back from making our dreams reality, is *an illusion*. In psychology corners, these illusions are referred to as "thinking errors," they are inaccuracies that we've been conditioned to believe – bugs in our brain's programming. Once we get familiar with what is *true and real*, and learn to utilize tools to conquer fear, a life without limits *becomes possible.*

To transform our self-doubt and anxiety, it's helpful to pause and dig deep enough to reveal the root of where it comes from. If you find yourself experiencing nervousness, self-doubt or anxiety at a barrel race, ask yourself – w*hy do I feel this way?* Then go deeper, peel back your reasoning like the layers of an onion. Ask yourself – *why,* again, or as many times as necessary. Do this until you feel as though you've reached the root cause of your self-doubt or anxiety.

Self-Doubt

Our self-image is made up of the mental pictures our brains store from all our collective experiences in life, starting when we were very young. Other people's judgments and opinions also play a part in developing this subconscious blue print of who we are and what we are capable of. Many of us may still carry the self image we developed in the distant past, allowing us to tap into only a small percentage of our ability. Our brains have basically been programmed to stay within a certain comfort zone, that is, our self-image. As with those stubborn riding habits, the brain identifies with what is familiar, and as neurons fire over time, they are attracted to the same "ruts" they have traveled for years.

Again, this may explain why some barrel racers seem to apply themselves in all the right areas, but really struggle with stepping up their performance in competition, no matter what they seem to do. This also explains why just when we're on the edge of a breakthrough, something happens to sabotage our success – we're pulled back onto the same pre-destined path.

What's very exciting and encouraging is that it *is possible* to send the bugs packing and reprogram our brain. Where we started does not have to determine where we end up. We hold the power to create *new* mental pictures and *new* neural pathways, to break free from the old ruts and create a *new* path that leads to the barrel racing success we desire.

Determine Your Desires

What changes are necessary to accomplish your desires in barrel racing? Get specific. What are the things you must be, do and have to make your desires reality? Develop an action plan – what must you learn, what specific actions must you take? Once you have a clear picture of where you want to go, ask yourself – *why?* Asking this question will help make sure you're desires are in alignment with your authentic self. Schedule time for your learning and action steps, protect that time and make it a top priority. Analyze your daily habits – do they take you closer or further away to achieving your barrel racing desires? Every day, do at least one thing that will get you closer to your desires.

Fear of Not Being Enough

One of the reasons so many of us experience self-doubt, anxiety or nervousness is because we (unconsciously) attach the results of competition to our worth. How we perform determines whether or not we feel good about ourselves. So when things go well, we're happy, and when they don't go as well, we experience a heavy dose of disappointment and discouragement.

This kind of attachment is a sure recipe for misery, as well as delayed success. The reality is that even barrel racers at the highest levels lose more than they win. There is no accomplishment in the world that will actually give you true self-worth. We are all valuable just because we ARE, not because of what we DO.

This doesn't mean we let go of our inner drive to excel, it just means our happiness is not based on our results. This also doesn't mean that we won't experience disappointment from time to time. The difference is that when we don't connect our results to our worth, we quickly transform it into inspiration to move to the next level. Disappointment is instead perceived as a sign telling us where to go and what to do next. Let go of the "I'll be happy when" mindset. The time to be content and happy is NOW and always, not when you reach some imaginary (ever moving) finish line, and not just when you win or perform well.

> 66 *Be happy now, without reason, or you never will be at all.* 99
>
> – Dan Millman

The Inner Critic

As you go forward on the journey toward mastering your inner game, a very large "bug" to watch out for is the whip-wielding inner critic. The inner critic can and will come out in full force on a regular basis and especially after a performance that we may have perceived as not up to par. Our inner critics will blow things out of proportion, over analyze, distort reality, jump to conclusions or apply labels and judgment. Inner critics feed on fear – they may be perfectionists or bullies that compare you to others, beat you up mentally and generally spread doom and gloom.

The conscious, left brain voices of the inner critic are inaccurate, and they interfere with our ability to use the right side of our brain. If we don't take serious effort to transform our inner critic into our inner wisdom, this bug will sabotage our success indefinitely.

When the inner critic pipes up, pause for a moment and ask yourself these two questions.

1. What is my inner critic saying?
2. What does my inner wisdom know as truth?

Once we become aware of these comments, we can start making effort to change. Initially, we may not realize the negative thinking has occurred until after the fact. Eventually, we'll make conscious changes in the moment. After catching the inner critic in the act for a while, we gradually start to create new neural pathways in our brain, for the positive thoughts of our inner wisdom to travel on, crowding out the inner critic. If we're committed to this process, eventually we'll become more like a "reverse paranoid," with a tendency toward seeing the good in every situation!

In the process of recognizing and correcting thinking errors, be gentle with yourself and don't allow your inner critic to use your new awareness as another excuse to mentally beat you up even more. Also keep in mind that due to the nature of the society in which we live, that preventing new fearful thoughts from taking hold in our minds will require ongoing effort.

What We Think About, We Bring About

We can be inspired to take more responsibility for our thoughts when we understand how the power of positive thinking works. The Law of Attraction is one of the better known universal laws. This metaphysical belief suggests that the energy we put out into the world is the kind we are going to attract back to us, and that we allow to occupy our minds is what becomes reality.

Before writing this off as "woo woo stuff," consider that many believe the theory to be very scientific. Science has found that everything in the world – our bodies, my laptop, your horse trailer, the gravel in the driveway, our horses, at the most microscopic level are made of vibrating molecules of energy.

Ever have one of those days when everything under the sun seems to go wrong? You may have sent out some bad vibes after the first few mishaps, and that keeps the 'ol ball rolling. Have you ever known of someone who complained constantly at restaurants and never seems to fail to receive poor food and service? "I always get bad service!" It's like a self-fulfilling prophecy. Negative thoughts attract negative results and positive thinking attracts positive results. Just like throwing a boomerang, the energy we transmit to the world, by way of our thoughts (conscious or not), will be returned to us, in the form of people and experiences with energy that are vibrating on similar frequencies.

> 66 *Your life is a reflection of your thoughts, if you change your thinking, you change your life.* 99
>
> — Brian Tracy

Watch Your Mouth

Just as important as monitoring our thoughts, is monitoring our words. Words also carry energy to either attract what we want or don't want. An example of a poor choice of words would be "Don't look at the barrel!" Our brains are unable recognize words like "don't" very well because of the tendency to operate like a mental dictionary of images. So what registers in our brain is "look at the barrel." If you decide to repeat an affirmation in your mind, by all means do so in a positive way, using words that describe what you do want, not what you don't want.

Every time you're about to make a negative thought, a negative comment, see if you can turn it around. Instead of saying "Don't look at the barrel," say "Keep your eyes up and looking forward." Replace "The ground here is always terrible!" with "I would like to see them do a better job with the ground." Instead of saying "He always drops his shoulder!" say "I think we need to work on elevating his shoulders." Replace "I can't stand suffering in this horrible heat!" with "The air will feel good when it cools down!" Words are spoken thoughts, and they hold great power, choose them wisely.

In addition, make it visual. Print out positive words that describe your desires, post them all over the house. Frame and hang specific words that represent your themes for the year. Use a combination of words and photos from magazines, from the internet, or even use favorite photos and make a vision board to represent your vision for the future. Consider making a rotating screen saver with images and words that represent your desires. Take advantage of the power mental imagery has to influence the subconscious mind.

Judgment

We all assign labels and judgments to ourselves, horses, other people, places – generally everything in our life to varying degrees. Many people are completely unaware both of this tendency and how, if we're not careful, it can negatively impact our lives and the lives of those around us. Whether we assign labels and judgments in our minds or out loud, we're creating another path to travel that we or whatever we're judging will have more tendency to stick to.

When it comes to negative judgments, it's most important to realize that the way in which we label others is actually a reflection of our opinions of ourselves. Talk about a wake-up call. If we are overly self-critical, we are very likely (whether we realize it or not) to be overly critical of everything around us. For many, labeling and judging is a form of avoidance. Looking deep within at our own issues is uncomfortable and sometimes scary – it's much easier to focus on others or anything external.

If you're feeling insecure, gossip and judgment might even give you a temporary, superficial high. You might feel a little better about yourself for a moment but this just breeds more self-criticism and less self-acceptance, sometimes even resulting in a "gossip hangover." When the initial high wears off, we really don't feel so great about assigning those negative judgments and labels to others. Develop a higher degree of awareness in your conversations in your own mind and with others. Build your own self-worth by avoiding negative labels and judgment of others.

> 66 *Great minds discuss ideas; average minds discuss events; small minds discuss people.* 99

– Eleanor Roosevelt

Without our interjection, the people, places, and things in our life just *are,* it's our opinions and thoughts that make them good or bad. There is much peace and contentment to be found in acceptance of ourselves and others, just as they are. This doesn't mean we don't strive for something different in our life, but we can do so without destructive negativity and criticism. When tempted, do your best to simply observe and recognize what *is*, instead of labeling.

Fear of Making a Mistake

As with any of the brands of fear mentioned in this chapter, the fear of making a mistake can over stimulate the left side of our brain, preventing the right side from functioning properly. When this occurs we experience what is referred to as "paralysis by analysis." Consider a person trying hard to thread a needle, the harder they focus on the task, the more they shake and the harder it becomes. When we fear making a mistake, we're so excessively careful and try so hard that we over think, sometimes actually causing us to freeze completely, unable to react appropriately, *or think*. A top barrel racing competitor is intensely focused, but rides in the moment with fluidity. Over thinking and trying too hard is the enemy of this. The result is poor timing, hesitation, abrupt movements and most certainly a slower time.

Overcoming this fear is possible with a simple change in perception that is possible through the realization that mistakes are not only important, but a necessary part of achieving success. Every failure can be turned around and perceived as one step closer to what we desire. The world's most successful people failed A LOT on their road to success.

> 66 *Every adversity, every failure, every heartache carries with it the seed of an equal or greater benefit.* 99
>
> – Napoleon Hill

When our performance doesn't go as planned, it's only an opportunity to look for a lesson and a gift, something we can learn and carry with us into the future. Consider the good points of each run, (there are always some) and how it felt, rather than judging your performance based strictly on the time. Develop an action plan including steps to take to avoid making the same mistake again.

Every mistake is one we never have to make again (thank goodness - like competing in a snap shirt with no tank top underneath). In addition to learning from your own mistakes, be open to learning from other people's mistakes (as I hope those did who were present the day I wore the snap shirt), it can fast forward your success exponentially. You don't always have to experience them directly to benefit!

Remember that our performance does not determine who we are, and we are not our mistakes. Winners see setbacks as only temporary and don't personalize them or make them permanent in their mind. Much like we must separate our worth from our accomplishments, we must also not define ourselves by our mistakes.

If you feel yourself trembling with anxiety caused by fear of making a mistake, think to yourself – what is the worst that could possibly happen? You might end up exactly where you were before you made that run, and would that be so bad? Could you live with that? When we are free of fear, we're more likely to realize that in the big scheme of things, a poor performance is really NOT the end of the world.

When you do make a mistake, step back and observe it rather than becoming critical. Visualize correcting the mistake in your mind. Trick your brain into not even realizing the mistake occurred, avoiding any resulting lack of confidence. The mind does not know the difference between real and vividly imagined events – use this to your advantage!

Fear of What Other People Think

The fear of what other people think is quite possibly one of the most common and crippling fears experienced by barrel racers. When this fear takes hold, you let who's watching determine how you ride, you might change your game plan based on what you're afraid someone will think, the fear of what others think may even influence major decisions. You might go out of your way to avoid certain people, all in an effort to look good in the eyes of others. You might over-analyze and obsess over things you said or did after the fact, thinking that maybe you gave the wrong impression, for fear of what others think.

"Be yourself; everyone else is already taken." – Oscar Wilde

These fearful, "what if" thoughts take up valuable space in our minds that could otherwise be filled with positive thoughts. When fearing what others think, we end up taking actions that sacrifice our authentic selves, in an effort to please someone on the outside. We'll even go to the extent of assuming that others are thinking negatively of us, in doing this, we're not only experiencing a thinking error, but we're attempting to put "bugs" in the minds of others. What we fear other people think is an illusion – they most likely don't even care!

This fear lives in close connection with the fear of not being enough. When we don't have confidence in ourselves, we seek affirmation of our worth on the outside to make up for what is lacking on the inside. If we truly accepted ourselves, it simply would not matter what other people thought of us.

To win the inner game of barrel racing, it's critical that we get in touch with our own authentic desires for our life and not allow something or someone on the outside to define them. We must release our attachment to what other people think and realize that we are enough, just because we are, not because of how much we win or someone else's opinion of us.

> 66 *The only fundamental rule for me is to just be yourself. Let your freak-flag fly, and if someone doesn't get you, move on.* 99
>
> – Drew Barrymore

This is not to say that you're not respectful and considerate of other people's time, space, and belongings because "you don't care what they think." You just don't allow your desire to look good in the eyes of others to consume your thoughts and control your actions. Free of this fear, you are empowered to live authentically and make decisions that are right for you and your horses. Nothing can shake that foundation of confidence deep within. If you find your concern for what others think influencing your little every day decisions, try replacing that with concern for what your horse thinks! You horse's opinion *does matter.*

Fly Your Flag

A fun example of this is a gal who barrel races locally. She has a habit of screaming, whooping and hollering throughout all her runs. She's not judged negatively for it, because she's secure with who she is. In fact, most spectators just laugh and scream along with her! She's loud and she's fun and she doesn't hold back. This barrel racer does not let what others think determine what works for her and her horses and is willing to go outside the box. In doing so, she is an inspiration! Her interesting combination of out of the ordinary techniques and extreme self-assuredness finds her often placing at the top of the results in the rodeos and barrel races she enters.

In Conclusion

Fear takes our power away, it influences and controls us. When fear has a hold on us, it's as if we are bound, we're held back from our greatest potential. Insecurities, self-doubt, anxiety and nervousness can only be a thing of the past when fear is a thing of the past.

Competing with horses has a way of bringing our weaknesses to light. We can look at it as an opportunity to develop strength, if we choose. When we're aware, we can notice where changes are necessary and take action. When we do, it can change everything – our relationships with horses, with people, and most importantly, with ourselves.

It's always possible to release subconscious fears instantly and permanently, but I would venture to say that this isn't how it happens for most people. It's more often released layer by layer though shifts in perception aided by an individual's personal commitment to growth. There are many books and programs that explain techniques and offer resources to assist in the release of subconscious fears. Remember that as you dive into learning materials, that there is a place for those resources, that they play an important part in your development as a barrel racer. Be mindful, however, that what you need to be a winner is already within you, it's just a matter of revealing what has been covered up. The experiences of life have a way of hiding your greatness within with negative, incorrect beliefs.

In the process of releasing and removing these attachments and fears, the blocks that get in the way of success; you develop better emotional fitness. As this happens, no matter the circumstances in *or* out of the arena, you become better able to keep things in perspective. You don't get rattled as easily and no longer project reflections of your insecurities on other people or on horses. You're not so much at the mercy of life's little challenges – they don't knock you off course like they used to.

When we release the fear of not being enough, the fear of making mistakes, the fear of what other people think, what is revealed is a rock solid, unbeatable foundation of confidence and security.

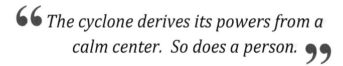 *The cyclone derives its powers from a calm center. So does a person.*

— Norman Vincent Peale

Tools & Techniques for Winning the Inner Game

- **Meditation** – Winning the inner game of barrel racing comes in large part through gaining the ability to quiet our inner monologue. This allows us to block out distractions and have laser-like focus only on those things in competition that are important to the task at hand. When letting go of the inner chatter box (who was never much good at coaching our way through a run and couldn't keep up anyway), our awareness heightens and we *feel* more than we think, we trust our mind and bodies and let them work to their potential.

One of the most direct lines to quieting the mind is through practicing meditation. Meditation is simply a process of emptying the mind of mental clutter. The clearness of mind and higher level of awareness that is achieved through meditation is the same type of mindful state that is desirable preceding and during a run. There are actually many psychological and physiological benefits to receive from a meditation practice. Some examples are relief from stress, greater creativity, enhanced energy, relaxation, release of tension in the body, improved self-confidence and an enhanced general state of well-being.

Consider developing a daily meditation practice (first thing in the morning is best). To start out, it might be very difficult to go twenty seconds without a conscious thought. As you build your mental muscles, it will become easier. At first, you might find it easiest to meditate in a perfectly calm, quiet environment. It might be helpful to play soothing music or listen to a pre-recorded guided meditation. Some guided meditation CD's I recommend are available on the Resources page at www.BarrelRacingTips.com. As you improve, try meditating when riding in the car or in environments that are more distracting. Eventually you'll be able to tune out distractions and achieve a clear state of mental focus and awareness that is precisely the type of mental state that benefits us most in competition.

- **Visualization** – The neurons that fire in our brains as we respond in a run, also fire when we visualize a run. Studies have shown that the brain does not recognize the difference between a real event and one that is vividly imagined. The more "vivid" our visualization, the better. So instead of just "seeing" or visualizing a run, instead *"sensualize"* your winning run, utilizing all your senses. Consider how much inner confidence you would gain if you visualized winning 100 rodeos in your mind! Visualization is like getting primed for competition, it links both hemispheres of the brain to work together and create your best performance. It's best, however, to utilize visualization to put your body and mind through the paces at home. When you get to the barrel race, put your mental efforts into breathing, focusing and quieting your mind.

Use the visualization below to improve your inner game:
Imagine several of the short go qualifiers have tipped barrels. Your performance in this run will determine whether you qualify for the National Finals Rodeo and create financial freedom and opportunity for rest and rejuvenation through the rest of the year. Over $50,000 is riding on the line. Years of preparation have come down to this very moment. You know what your horse is capable of and he is performing at peak level. With your body relaxed and your mind quiet, begin to visualize images of your performance. There are several knobs in front of you. Reach for the first knob and use it to enlarge your mental picture. Everything you see is three dimensional. As you turn the second knob, you brighten and enhance the colors in your picture. Everything you see is becoming even more brilliant. Next, turn up the volume. The sounds you hear become crisp and clear. Imagine every movement, even the tiniest details. You see yourself gathering your reins in both hands. You blast down the alley and push aggressively to the first barrel. The approach is perfect, your turn quick and correct. You sprint to second and your horse uses his hind end in one smooth cougar-type "whoosh" motion. You are completely in tune with him and use your body language subtly to guide him. You set up for the third in perfect position, finish the turn fluidly and race for home. The crowd cheers as you have posted the new fast time. You hear your name loudly announced as the new leader. Imagine the emotions you feel after making that perfect run. Imagine rubbing your horse on the neck, "GOOD BOY!" and the pride you feel in your heart. Feel your chest swell and your eyes well up as you realize that your hard work and commitment is paying off. See yourself

walking him out with a big smile on your face. Friends and people you don't even know come to congratulate you, everyone around you says "Good RUN!" You smile and say thank you, with tears still welling up. You and your horse are whisked away for photos with your gigantic check, saddle and other prizes. You are filled with so much gratitude to be living the life of your dreams.

Replay these images over and over. Consider using a mobile phone or free software such as Audacity (download at www.Audacity.SourceForge.net) to record your own voice reading these words, than saving for playback as an MP3 on your iPod or iPhone, if you have one. Rather than imagining, you can also perform a "success history search" and go back mentally to any big wins or positive experiences you've actually had that you would mentally benefit from experiencing over and over. Study, absorb and enjoy these sensualization experiences. Maximize your senses; the key is to make your images as clear, detailed and vivid as you can.

- **Breathing to Relax the Body and Quiet the Mind** – Breathing techniques are very valuable when it comes to achieving a quiet mind and easing pre-race anxiety. Preceding your run, even as you are warming up your horse, count to four as you gently take a slow and even breath through your nose (30% of air goes straight to the brain when air is inhaled through the nose). Allow your belly to comfortably expand as you fill up your lungs. Hold the breath for a count of six. For added relaxation, form a fist with one hand and hold it as you hold your breath. Next, exhale slowly and allow the air to be fully expelled from the lungs as you count to seven. When you exhale, open and relax your fist as you release any tension from your body. Repeat. Counting as you breathe helps focus your mind's attention rather than allowing it to be distracted by your environment.

- **Get into Character** – To BE and embody the person you want to be, fake it until you make it! If you're plagued by self-doubt, start taking actions and treating yourself as a valuable person and eventually your subconscious beliefs will start to align with your actions. Watch videos of your role models. Lift your head and direct your eyes straight in front of you, put a grin on your face, pull your shoulders back and begin breathing deep and rhythmically. Emulate the best – you are Charmayne James (or whatever role model you choose). Take a moment to think about Charmayne, an 11 time world champion barrel racer who you respect and admire. As you think about her, concentrate on how she performs. Specifically notice the expression on her face, her body posture, and the attitude and aura she carries into the arena. Study this athlete carefully. Imagine yourself taking on those characteristics that you've identified with this athlete.

- **Mental Reprogramming** - To take our mental game to the highest level, we must trust our right brain functioning. We must first make sure we have done the homework necessary to develop our right brain abilities so this functioning CAN be trusted in a run.

    If you have a particularly well established riding habit that you seem to revert to in a run and is no longer serving you, then specific visualizations that are customized and involve you sensualizing what you want to replace that habit with can make all the difference. If you're serious about kicking a bad riding habit, make your visualization as realistic as possible by riding your horse at a walk around an imaginary barrel pattern with your eyes closed as you visualize yourself riding perfectly. Commit to doing this for 15 minutes every day for 30 days, and prepare to be amazed at the results in your next competition.

When it comes to fully trusting our right brain to help us react appropriately, there are blocks that can get in the way, all of which have been covered in preceding sections of this book. Make sure you develop yourself in other areas of horsemanship as well, so that your abilities compliment, rather than interfere with and inhibit each other.

66 *A dream is in the mind of the believer and in the hands of the doer. You are not given a dream without being given the power to make it come true.* 99

— Anonymous

The #1 Secret

To add some diversity to my home environment as a child, I would often spend time building massive, intricate forts in the shelter belt of trees near my home. I drug heavy scraps of wood, bricks, even old pieces of furniture through the pasture to construct these forts. They consisted of "rooms" both on the ground and up in the trees. Of course, I was always on the lookout in various junk piles for things to add to my forts as well. When I didn't have a drill, I'd pound a hole in a piece of wood with a small nail. When I didn't have a hammer, I used a piece of scrap metal to pound nails. I used an old, dull saw meant for small branches to cut pieces of plywood, and it would sometimes take hours. If I had had other options available to me, or power tools, I certainly would have used them. (Of course I don't advocate the use of dull hand tools *or* power tools to any eight year old child.) The construction process was the farthest thing from easy, in fact it was very difficult, but that never turned me off. I would create a beautiful, peaceful oasis with the materials I had available, constantly thinking of new ways in which to improve what I already had.

I have never failed to be amazed at what could be created through being driven, innovative and resourceful, even without all the tools that one would assume to be necessary for accomplishing a certain task or goal. Never one to throw my hands in the air, today my husband lovingly refers to me as a "female MacGyver."

At times it may seem like the valuable bits of information and insights necessary to reach the highest levels of barrel racing competition are few and far between. Discovering the secrets to barrel racing success is not always easy. The world's most successful barrel racers, however, aren't turned off or discouraged when things are *not easy*. Although certain aspects of the search may prove difficult, I guarantee, it will always be worthwhile.

To experience success you've never had, you must be willing to do what you've never done – to peel back the layers and reveal the real underlying reasons for your challenges. Your achievement in barrel racing is determined by your willingness to do the work, *even when it's hard.* It comes though balancing that powerful desire which propels you forward with an inner knowing of when to pause, say "wait, this *shouldn't* be so hard," and go back to the drawing board.

Success comes in large part, through knowing *where* to look for those missing pieces. It comes especially through the realization that barrel racing is more about self-development than it is horse training. Success comes, not necessarily from finding the right technique, the right horse, or the right tack, but with the awareness to recognize and dissolve blocks in the way of the success *that is already possible.*

When it comes to horses, I will never claim to have *all* the answers. There is so much yet to learn. What I do have is an insatiable curiosity and desire to propel forward, much like I did in my fort building days. True dedication to never-ending self-development means being willing to ask the same questions every day without assuming you already know the answer. When something isn't working, go searching, without a doubt that you will find what's missing. As you do, you'll realize how satisfying and fulfilling it is to discover those missing pieces — perfect additions to your own barrel racing masterpiece.

> ❝ *The important thing is to not stop questioning.* ❞
>
> — Albert Einstein

What I have now, in addition to that forward drive that I didn't have previously, is more acceptance for what *is*. I've developed a better ability to sit back and enjoy what I have built. It's made my current journey less frantic, allowing me to be in the moment and simply feel, which has actually fast forwarded my progress on this journey exponentially. Sometimes we have to slow down to speed up, in life and in barrel racing. This way of being has given me a better ability to sense where my efforts really should be focused to be most effective. What I've created is beautiful as it is, but I'm always open, receptive and willing to add to it.

Do what you can with what you've got, even if it's a 32 year old trailer and a 22 year old, 14 hand Appaloosa!

After all I overcame as a youngster, any obstacle seems real small in comparison to those I face today. In some sense, although my past experiences contributed to many blocks in the way of my success, on some level it also instilled a fearlessness – an inner knowing that I really can start with nothing, and create something completely miraculous.

On the day the photo above was taken, I pulled into a barrel race with my 32 year old Stidham two-horse trailer and unloaded my 22 year old mare, my only horse at the time. We left the barrel race that day with a trophy buckle. The lesson here is that you might not always feel like you have what it takes to rise to the top in barrel racing.

The truth is — it doesn't matter.

Regardless of where we start, we all face different types of challenges. Take what you've been blessed with and develop it to the best of your ability, and you'll continue to be blessed with more. I knew that if I kept trying, kept moving forward, was willing to try new things, willing to throw out what didn't work, was willing to shift my perceptions, that I could overcome the odds and create something amazing, with horses or anything else. The same is true for you.

> ❝ *Life is ten percent what happens to you and ninety percent how you respond to it.* ❞
>
> — Lou Holtz

There comes a time after all the homework, preparation and learning that we just get in the zone and let go of the performance and the results, and our illusion of control; we surrender the outcome to a power greater than ourselves, a power we know always has our best interest in mind, a power we can trust. I believe that we are created with desires in our hearts and given certain talents as gifts. I also believe that horses are placed in our lives as gifts. Acting upon your desires, using your talents and caring for your horses are the best ways in which to show appreciation for these gifts.

Protect the foundational love of horses that drew you to barrel racing to begin with. Refuse to let any kind of fear, insecurity or any other type of block stand in the way of your wildest barrel racing dreams. You were not put on this earth to hold back. Utilize your talents by putting it all on the line in competition and otherwise, without hesitation. You were intended to shine bright, in the arena and out. Think, speak and act with love and acceptance, and watch as fear, insecurity, self-doubt and anxiety dissolve. Set an example by putting an end to complaining, gossiping, judging yourself or others, and start loving and lifting others from the bottom up. We can only reveal in our horses what we first have within ourselves. When you place your focus on being an amazing person, being an amazing barrel racer comes naturally.

We are all meant for greatness, and when you reveal your own, you inspire others to do the same. What's created in the process is a new enthusiasm and appreciation for barrel racing and for life in general. It's a weight lifted – suddenly there is more fun and ease and less worry. Rather than being driven by fear, you realize it's that power greater than yourself working through you that makes it all possible. You realize that you really can achieve extraordinary things, and that every little step along the way is extraordinary in itself. Your wins and losses are all blessings, you accept each of them with humility and gratitude for the opportunities they present to learn and grow.

> I'd like to share the story of two farmers. Both farmers desperately needed rain. They both prayed for rain, but only one went out and prepared his fields to receive it. Which one do you think trusted God to send the rain? Of course, the one who prepared his fields. Which one are you? Set a positive expectation by having faith and trusting that your barrel racing success will come when the time is right. Until then, be willing to accept guidance and do your best in preparation to receive success. Do the work, but surrender the outcome.

The secret to barrel racing success is found through extending your love for horses and barrel racing to everything and everyone around you. It's in never giving up and having an insatiable desire to keep "preparing your fields," and dissolving the blocks that get in the way of realizing that at the deepest level, you have everything you need to win, already within you. When you fully receive and utilize your God-given gifts as a reflection of gratitude, you will appreciate the wins that take place each and every day, regardless of what happens in the arena.

These, are the *Secrets to Barrel Racing Success.*

66 *Somewhere behind the barrel racer you've become,*
the hours of riding, the horses you've pushed,
and the horses that pushed you,
and your parents and fans who cheer for you,
is the little girl who fell in love with a horse,
and never looked back... Ride for her. 99

— Unknown

Resources

As you navigate your individual path to achieving barrel racing success, I've mentioned that it's critical that you don't overlook the well of resources that already exist within you; although, outer resources and experiences do play a big part in our growth, and can actually facilitate the process of revealing the winner within.

I'd be doing you a disservice if I didn't share some ideas for increasing the odds that you'll continue to find those rare bits of insight on your journey that can make all the difference. As you expose yourself to new information, consider its source, weigh it all in and trust yourself to sort out what resonates and is worthy of taking action on, and what is not.

Research the Internet – Though simple utilization of Google, you're likely to find helpful information on any topic under the sun, even on specific horsemanship and/or barrel racing subjects. Articles and videos abound – take advantage of the learning opportunities always available at your fingertips on the internet. Especially consider utilizing online forums specifically for barrel racers. Ask questions and receive input from other barrel racers who have gone before you and may have already found a solution to the problem you're experiencing. Find the web sites of one or several trainers or clinicians (barrel racing or otherwise) that you align with. Sign up for their newsletters, membership clubs or purchase their educational materials.

Make Local Contacts – Ask around to get opinions on trainers in your area, schedule lessons with them or offer to help exercise horses in return for lessons. Even if someone doesn't advertise as offering lessons, doesn't mean you can't ask or that they might not be happy to help you. Consider riding with successful trainers, even in other disciplines. Your barrel horse is likely to benefit immensely from cross training. Visit with a local professional barrel racer that you admire and ask if you can travel to rodeos with them. Success leaves clues, study the habits of the successful people you admire.

> **❝** *Don't wait for someone to take you under their wing. Find a good wing and climb up underneath it.* **❞**
>
> — Frank C. Bucaro

Offer to help with chores and of course pay your way. Whether you bring your own horse and enter or not, you're likely to benefit just from sharing the same air as someone who has climbed the ladder of barrel racing success.

Read – To prevent information overload, start by determining any areas in which you'd like to learn more. Think about the areas where your horse needs improvement or where you have some weak areas in your own foundation of knowledge and focus on those areas. As you read books and articles pertaining to barrel horse training, consider studying different aspects of horse health, horsemanship, and even general self-development. Readers are leaders, the most valuable tool you have to achieve greatness is right between your ears – exercise it regularly. For a collection of recommended books and more, visit the Resources page at www.BarrelRacingTips.com.

DVD's – Ask your friends what horse training DVDs they have in their collection and offer to trade. There are numerous instructional barrel racing DVDs available and a limitless number of DVDs created by highly qualified horsemanship clinicians. Take notes when you watch DVDs and keep them organized so you can refer back and refresh your memory in an instant. Consider subscribing to a horse training video rental service such as

GiddyUpFlix (www.GiddyUpFlix.com), which is like NetFlix for horse lovers.

Clinics – Find out about all types of horsemanship clinics that are available in your area. Audit or participate in as many as you can, even if they aren't focused on the discipline of barrel racing. Even if you don't resonate with all the ideas presented, you're likely to take something of value away from every professional horseman you come in contact with. Take detailed notes at these clinics. If you're riding in a clinic, when you make shifts in your horsemanship, really memorize the FEEL, so you can take that home as well.

Library – Yes, you can find great resources to add to your horsemanship foundation at the good 'ol local library! What I especially recommend though, is creating your own library at home. Keep anything valuable you come across, such magazine articles, inspirational quotes, notes from clinics or DVDs. Organize it all into binders that you can always refer to at a moment's notice. Our brains simply aren't designed to hold and keep all the information we are presented with. When you experience an issue or just want to study up, you'll always have a great selection of materials on hand to refer to.

Subscriptions – A magazine subscription to Barrel Horse News is simply a must have for any barrel racer. There is nothing that compares to the educational articles available in this publication. Also visit www.BarrelHorseNews.com to subscribe to their email lists to receive articles that are not available in the print magazine. In addition, consider subscribing to The Barrel Racing Report (www.BarrelRacingReport.com), a free weekly barrel racing email newsletter that contains results, barrel race entry information, and insider interviews with the nation's tops barrel racers.

Video Review – Consider contacting those professionals you respect and offer to pay them for a video critique, or submit your barrel racing video at www.WatchMyRun.com, a website designed for barrel racers to submit videos of their runs for professionals to watch and critique for a fee. You can also upload videos to YouTube – ask your friends to have a look, or ask people on barrel racing forums to give you pointers. Often times, we just don't have *eyes to see* issues in our own runs that might be obvious to someone else; it's a great way to develop new awareness and discover problem areas you never knew existed.

Ask, Ask, Ask – A question not asked is a door not opened! Never hold back questions – doing so is usually a sign of fear and insecurity. Never fail to ask for clearer understanding at a clinic or in a lesson. Your teachers want you to understand and succeed. At a barrel race, ask your friends to watch your run and let you know how they think it can be improved. There's always a chance they might only tell you what you already know, but how do you know unless you ask? Offer to pay a professional barrel racer you admire to watch your run and critique you afterwards. Most people are complimented when you ask their advice. Make sure there is something in it for the other person and make it a win, win.

66 *Ask for what you want. Ask for help, ask for input, ask for advice and ideas — but never be afraid to ask.* 99

— Brian Tracy

Are You Ready?

Do you and your horse have the foundations in place to be a competitive team? Take the fun quiz below to find out. Circle your answer to each question and add up your score at the end.

1. If you asked your horse to sprint then stop it would look something like this...

    A) We would take a few seconds to reach top speed, and we would definitely want to have a wall or fence to help us stop

    B) My horse will accelerate well but once he gets going, he would rather keep going, it takes a few seconds and some pulling to get him stopped

    C) My horse can accelerate and reach top speed almost instantly and he is so in tune to my body language that he'll transition down to a stop just as quickly

2. You're getting ready at the barrel race and notice something unusual...

    A) Your horse seemed stiff the minute he stepped out of the trailer, you called the barrel race producer to draw out, then headed to the vet. clinic so you could get your horse on the road to recovery ASAP

    B) Some lady waved at you, then came over to tell you that your horse is moving very short strided like something is wrong, she says maybe he's tying up, you wonder what that means and ride away

    C) You thought your horse felt strange, you get off, lunge him and confirm he is short striding and decide to draw out, no sense taking a risk

3. When you ask your horse to yield his shoulder, rib cage or hip with leg pressure he responds...

   A) Really well at a standstill, and pretty good at a trot
   B) It's hit or miss, sometimes he steps over, sometimes he ignores me
   C) My horse will position his body pretty much anywhere, at any time, we can perform lateral movements at a walk, trot and lope

4. When you close your eyes and vividly imagine yourself making a run *bareback,* you...

   A) Know for sure you would fall off at the first barrel, if not sooner
   B) Think it would be challenging but could do it if you practiced
   C) Would feel ready to enter if there was a bareback division at the next barrel race

5. At a trot, when you softly pick up the reins and encourage your horse forward with your body's energy, your horse...

   A) Softly flexes at the poll and gathers into a springy but smooth trot
   B) Pushes his nose against the rein pressure and keeps going
   C) Slows down or stops, he knows that rein pressure means "whoa" no matter what my body is doing

6. After spending time with your horse, how does he respond when you put him back in his pen/pasture?

   A) He takes off at a gallop
   B) He hangs around, hoping that he'll get a scratch
   C) He leaves at a brisk walk to join his buddies

7. Your horse is still healing from an injury and your barrel buddy calls saying her and another friend are going to a big barrel race in a month and it will be really fun, you're invited...

   A) You say you'll go, but opt to leave your horse home, that way he can have time to heal and you can still have fun with your friends
   B) You say you'll go, start riding your horse right away, even if he's not totally healed, the competition will be way too much fun to miss out on!
   C) You stay home, thinking about how you'll never get to barrel race and generally feel left out

8. When you ask your horse to flex his body, and walk in a circle at the same time he...

   A) Is able to keep moving forward, but bends mostly at his neck, he can walk in a circle but his body is mostly straight
   B) Really struggles with maintaining flexion and moving forward at the same time, he's kind of all over the place
   C) Is able to shape his body on the circle, stay softly flexed through his body and moving forward

9. When your horse comes to a stop at the gate after a barrel run your body position...

   A) Is a little forward and gripping with my legs but with a secure seat
   B) Secure and seated deep in the saddle, my body is leaning back slightly
   C) My butt bounces off the saddle a little bit and sometimes I worry that if my horse turned suddenly I would fall off

10. When you approach your horse to halter him, how are you greeted?

A) My horse usually has his butt toward me, ignoring me

B) My horse usually leaves when he sees me coming with a halter

C) My horse walks half way to meet me, approaching me face first

11. When holding the reins in your hands...

A) It feels like I have to pull and jerk sometimes to get anything accomplished

B) I feel my horses mouth and he feels my hands, I follow his movement and try not to bump his mouth by accident, he stays within the lines of communication

C) Sometimes the contact with my horse's mouth feels soft, but I have to be firm quite often also

12. Your friend's invite you to go out for dinner and drinks after the barrel race. You're tired and you haven't finished all your horse chores and you have exhibitions early in the morning, you...

A) Decline the invite but appreciate it and say you'll join them next time, instead you cold hose your horses legs, massage him, take him for a walk then go to bed early

B) Throw some hay, fill the water bucket and jump in. You stay out late and end up missing your exhibitions in the morning

C) Stay with your horse but are kind of rude to him because you're resentful that his need for extra care got in the way of your fun

13. When asking your horse to trot from a stand still...

A) He will trot off with leg pressure but sometimes he volunteers to go faster or he breaks down to a walk without getting the cue to do so

B) I always wear spurs so my horse knows I mean business, if he doesn't trot or breaks out of a trot, I kick him

C) I just lift the reins and apply subtle leg pressure and he goes off at a brisk trot and stays trotting until I ask otherwise

14. Your promising, young horse ducked out at the barrel and took you on a wild ride back to the gate...

A) You're so embarrassed that you can't make any eye contact when you go out the gate, you are almost in tears, when you exit the arena you jerk on your horse's mouth, and consider putting a "for sale" ad up online when you get home

B) You are concerned because you know that you've put such a solid foundation in your horse that there must be something very seriously wrong with him physically and are determined to fix the issue

C) You are very frustrated and question whether your horse is cut out for barrel racing, you really work him hard after the run and at home during the next two weeks

15. When asking your horse to pick up the right lead...

A) You lift your energy, apply light pressure with your opposite leg and your horse always seems to position himself correctly to take the correct lead

B) You apply pressure with your opposite leg but sometimes he picks up the wrong one

C) You're not positive what lead you're on or how to ask for one or the other, and when you start loping, it's either rushed or takes a few trotting steps to get going

16. When you are loping and then exhale, relax and sit deep in the saddle and say "whoa," your horse...

A) Stops eventually after a few rough trotting steps
B) Keeps going at a lope without much regard to my body language
C) Melts into a smooth stop

17. When you go out to feed you notice what looks like minor swelling in both your horses front legs, he hasn't been kept in a stall and shouldn't be stocked up, you...

A) Hope that it's nothing and that it's just hard to tell whether there is swelling or not because of his winter hair, you make a note to check them after work tomorrow
B) Are certain something is up, you know your horses legs like the back of your hand so you put ice boots on them and schedule a vet. appointment for first thing in the morning
C) Don't worry about it, he probably caught his leg in a panel, you figure the swelling will resolve on its own

18. At the barrel race, you notice the horse that is tied up next to yours is kicking or pulling back, you...

A) Politely let the horse's owner know that her horse is pulling back or kicking, saying that you were concerned he could get hurt, you keep an eye on your horse and move him if necessary

B) Decide to move your horse, it's just not worth risking yours getting hurt, you give the other horse's owner a dirty look and complain about her to your friend

C) Find the horse's owner, and (loudly) give her a piece of your mind for leaving her misbehaving horse unattended

19. In a run, if your horse drops on his front end or leans into a turn...

   A) There's not much I can do about it when it happens
   B) He resists me for a second but I can move him over with my leg and reins if I am firm enough
   C) I can change his body position instantly because he's responsive to my cues even with speed

20. You were running late for the barrel race, forgot your favorite headstall, and then got a flat tire on the way. By the time you arrive, they are only 20 riders away from your run, you...

   A) Scream, cry, have a meltdown, slam the trailer door, give your mom or husband orders to help you and think that all this may even be their fault
   B) Think there's nothing like living in the fast lane! You realize your troubles are minor and vow to be better prepared next time, you stay focused on your run and your horse seems to fire even harder with less warm up
   C) The stress of being rushed and worry of not having the right head gear gets to you mentally, you're able to get ready for your run barely in time but you're mentally shaken up and don't perform your best

21. If you focused on a fence post in the arena, dropped your reins and asked your horse to trot to it…

    A) He would trot in a perfectly straight line until I asked him to stop with his head in line with the post

    B) We'd get to the post eventually, but he'd probably miss being in line with it by about a foot and he'd probably swerve around a little on the way there

    C) He'd turn around and start heading out the gate on his own if I wasn't holding the reins

22. You would like to bring your young horse along to the barrel race for the experience, so you…

    A) Take him with, ride him and tell everyone you see that he's young and you haven't had time for him, so that people know you have a good excuse for having such an unruly horse

    B) Decide not to because his behavior would make you look like an idiot

    C) Bring him to the arena with you next week instead to more gradually transition him to going places and be sure to work with him in the days in between, you care more about what your horse thinks and feels than what other people do

23. You and your horse are eligible to win a season-ending championship, two weeks before the barrel race he comes up lame…

    A) Have him injected and keep riding, you worked hard and are going to make sure you have a chance at winning

    B) Give him some time off, and have your race track friend look at him, you do some special body therapies and exercise him a few times before the race so you are able to compete

C) Based on your assessment, you decide to haul him long distance to the veterinary teaching hospital where they find out it's a tear in a ligament that will take months to heal, you are grateful to have an accurate diagnosis, so he has a chance at full recovery

24. When you close your eyes and vividly imagine what it would feel like riding without reins, or without arms you...

A) Think it would be fun
B) Feel afraid, there is no way you could stop your horse without reins or arms
C) Feel like it would be very challenging to use other parts of your body for communication and balance

25. Your horse starts to show symptoms of colic in the middle of the night at the barrel race...

A) You notice in the morning that he's sweaty and that he has made a mess of his stall but go forward with your regular routine
B) You're glad your name and phone number is posted on his stall, you were awaken by a call on your cell phone when someone noticed him rolling
C) You know for certain that your horse normally doesn't paw or roll, and that it's too cool for him to be sweating, you call a vet. in the morning and decide not to run and jeopardize your horse's health

26. You've been working all day and have a barrel race coming up this weekend, the weather is cold and windy...

A) You succumb to the temptation to snuggle up and watch a movie but vow to exercise your horse the rest of the week, although you haven't checked the weather forecast yet

B) You realize your horse might not focus very well in the inclement weather anyway so go out and spend some quality time with him in the barn, then watch a training video or visit BarrelRacingTips.com for any new tips

C) The weather isn't good the rest of the week either, so your horse is just going to have to get by without much exercise, it's also too cold to mess with feeding your horse his supplements

27. After you've haltered your horse, how does he respond to going with you?

A) He stays by my side and seems generally happy to be going with me

B) He lags behind and is generally not very eager to move

C) He pulls me aside to snatch bites of grass, and sometimes tugs on the lead rope or invades my space when startled or excited

28. At the barrel race, you and your friends talk about...

A) How poor the ground conditions are and how the barrel race producer is always late

B) How incompetent other people are, you make fun of them, laugh and gossip over the juicy details of their personal lives

C) The new things you've learned lately, you give other people compliments whether you know them or not, you laugh and have fun, without it being at the expense of others

29. You notice the dips behind your horse's shoulders are getting bigger and that your horse seems very cranky when you saddle him, you...

    A) Don't think much of it, he's always been cinchy and lots of horses have those dips behind the shoulders
    B) Ask your horse chiropractor what he thinks about it next time you see him
    C) Do some research on saddle fit and determine that without a doubt, that poor saddle fit is not only making your horse uncomfortable and causing muscle atrophy but it could be interfering with his performance

30. When performing slow work on the barrel pattern...

    A) You notice your horse's body position is a little off and he's taking a step outside the specific path he knows to follow, you do some dry work away from the pattern to explore the issue further and realize after freeing up his shoulder, the issue seems resolved
    B) Didn't notice your horse was getting out of position or off track in slow work, he starts blowing off turns in runs so you jerk on him and call him stupid
    C) After a few sessions on the barrels you finally notice that something is not right with your horse, you spend a few more days trying to troubleshoot it but aren't really sure what the problem is and think about calling an equine chiropractor

1. A = 2, B = 1, C = 3
2. A = 1, B = 2, C = 3
3. A = 3, B = 1, C = 2
4. A = 2, B = 1, C = 3
5. A = 3, B = 1, C = 2
6. A = 1, B = 3, C = 2
7. A = 3, B = 1, C = 2
8. A = 2, B = 1, C = 3
9. A = 2, B = 3, C = 1
10. A = 1, B = 2, C = 3
11. A = 1, B = 3, C = 2
12. A = 3, B = 1, C = 2
13. A = 2, B = 1, C = 3
14. A = 1, B = 3, C = 2
15. A = 3, B = 2, C = 1

16. A = 2, B = 1, C = 3
17. A = 2, B = 3, C = 1
18. A = 3, B = 2, C = 1
19. A = 1, B = 2, C = 3
20. A = 1, B = 3, C = 2
21. A = 3, B = 2, C = 1
22. A = 2, B = 1, C = 3
23. A = 1, B = 2, C = 3
24. A = 3, B = 1, C = 2
25. A = 1, B = 3, C = 2
26. A = 2, B = 3, C = 1
27. A = 3, B = 2, C = 1
28. A = 2, B = 1, C = 3
29. A = 1, B = 2, C = 3
30. A = 3, B = 1, C = 2

Total 1 – 15 _____

Total 16 – 30 _____

+

Total 1 – 15 _____

=

Grand Total _____

30–45 – Develop a solid foundation in your horse and in yourself as a rider before running barrels, and you'll get a lot further, a lot faster.

45–60 – Find out where the "holes" are in your barrel racing program, and fill them in before going further on the barrels.

60–75 – Keep up the good work, keep learning and you're well on your way.

75–90 – See you at the NFR!

About the Author

Little did she know where such humble beginnings with a renegade 14 hand Appaloosa would take her. Today Heather Smith is living her dream. She can be found at the arena, training and maintaining her barrel horses, on the road competing with them, or in her home office, sharing what she learns through her experiences.

Over the years, Heather has overcome a number of obstacles that stood in the way of barrel racing success. Lessons were often hard earned, which is why she is enthusiastic to pave a road for other barrel racers that features fewer hardships and more ease. Although she has successfully trained for and competed in reining events, and has extensive experience with colt starting and rehabilitating troubled horses, barrel racing continues to be Heather's primary focus.

Perhaps what sets Heather apart is her unbridled enthusiasm for learning. This passion inspires her to create and take advantage of opportunities to learn from the best in the industry. Heather has worked closely and ridden extensively with, attended and/or participated in numerous clinics taught by the well known trainers, clinicians and professionals listed below:

- Buck Brannaman
- Ray Hunt
- Marlene McRae
- Lynn McKenzie
- Les Vogt
- Clinton Anderson
- Charmayne James
- Gary Leffew
- Kay Blandford

- Lynn Kohr
- Ed Wright
- Dave Ellis
- George Williamson
- Jane Melby
- Molly Powell
- Lisa Lockhart
- Kristi Smith

In addition, Heather has invested a great deal of time and resources developing her education on the specific topics of equine massage, chiropractic, nutrition and natural hoof care. She holds an Associate of Applied Science Degree in Veterinary Technology and maintains licensure as a Veterinary Technician.

Heather's experiences have led her to realize that achieving success in barrel racing, or any discipline, is really more about self-development than it is horse training, and that only when we reveal the best in ourselves, can we do the same with horses.

Through her own experiences, she's become determined to make the critical but lesser-known secrets to barrel racing success more understandable and readily available to barrel racers around the world. Today, she does just that through her web site – www.BarrelRacingTips.com where she offers quality, original how-to articles and Q&A videos as well as a collection of information products designed specifically for those barrel racers who are ready and willing to take their competition to the next level.

Visit www.BarrelRacingTips.com to sign up for free winning tips via email.

Connect on Facebook at www.Facebook.com/BarrelRacingTips.

0570

53052719R00103

Made in the USA
Lexington, KY
19 June 2016